I AM
AMAZING

A No-Nonsense Self Love Guide To Remember
Your Greatness And Rock Out Your Life!

PETRA EATJUICY

I AM AMAZING

This book is to activate your empowerment, deep inner knowing and radical self love. No part of this book diagnosis or prescribes anything. All visions inside this book are the author's beliefs and views. You are free to choose if want to take on any of the ideas in this book. You are a sovereign free powerful amazing soul. This book is to remind you of that. Petra is not a doctor and not claiming to be. She is a teacher and a guide.

May you be inspired, empowered, educated and enlightened reading these words. May you be more of you!

ISBN (978-1521890684)

Cover design by Poli Peeva & Petra EatJuicy
Book Design by Ina Kuehfuss & Petra EatJuicy

Visit me on the web!
www.EatJuicy.com
www.GreenSmoothieGangster.com

Tell me how you liked the book!
www.Facebook.com/PetraEatJuicyTV

First Edition: 2017

For the
UNIVERSAL DIVINE FEMININE CREATOR ENERGY
that has long been laying dormant inside all humans,
waiting for this time to emerge
and save the world

AND

For my MOMMA who got her
angel wings way too early,
perhaps if she only knew what is in this book
she would still be here

CONTENTS

HEY SUPER HUMAN!
YES YOU!
I'M NO SUPER HUMAN - YOU MIGHT SAY
OH YES YOU ARE
YOU ARE A POWERFUL HUMAN ON THIS PLANET
FULL OF SUPER POWERS
AND YOU ARE SUPER POWERFUL!
YOU MIGHT HAVE FORGOTTEN
THAT'S OK. I'M HERE TO REMIND YOU
THAT'S WHY YOU HAVE THIS BOOK TO REMEMBER
WHY DO YOU WANT TO BE REMEMBER?
BECAUSE LIVING LIFE IN YOUR FULL POWER
TOTALLY IN LOVE WITH YOURSELF
IS WAY MORE FUN
YOU MIGHT THINK YOU LIKE YOURSELF
BUT DO YOU LOVE AND ADORE YOURSELF?
CAN YOU SEE YOUR OWN GREATNESS?
CAN YOU SEE YOUR POTENTIAL AS A POWERFUL HUMAN
ON THIS PLANET?
I'LL SHOW YOU HOW....I'LL SHINE MY LIGHT
TO GIVE YOU PERMISSION TO SHINE YOURS
LIFE IS GREAT AND IT CAN BE BETTER
I WILL REMIND YOU OF YOUR SUPER POWERS TO
MAKE LIFE EVEN BETTER
YOU ARE HERE TO MAKE A FOOTPRINT OF CHANGE,
INSPIRATION AND LOVE
YOU ARE HERE ON THIS PLANET FOR A REASON
YOUR LIFE HAS MEANING
YOU ARE MIRACLE

YOU ARE POWERFUL

YOU ARE AMAZING

YOU ARE STRONG

YOU ARE BRAVE

YOU ARE REALLY, REALLY SMART

YOU ARE LOVEABLE

YOU ARE LOVED

YOU ARE LOVED BY THE UNIVERSE

YOU ARE LOVED BY EVERYONE

YOU ARE SPECIAL

YOU ARE A SHINING BRIGHT LIGHT FOR SO MANY PEOPLE

YOU ARE EXCEPTIONAL

YOU ARE EXTRAORDINARY

YOU ARE GOOD LOOKING, BEAUTIFUL, STUNNING

YOU ARE CLEVER

YOU ARE ENOUGH

YOU ARE ENOUGH

YOU ARE ENOUGH

...

A Love Note From Petra

HEY SUPER HUMAN WELCOME! I AM EXCITED you are here! You are fabulous! Right now, right here. You are fabulous! You have everything you need to be fully happy in your life or to change your circumstance so that you are. Only you can do this. Only you can bring more joy and love into your life. Only you can truly declare your own personal power. Only you can be in charge of your own life.

So how are things? Are you happy and fulfilled? Do you feel comfortable in your skin and love who you are? How are you in relationships? How are you at communication? Are you sometimes struggling in your human existence? Does life get you down and do you feel alone in the world? Do you feel suppressed by outside forces and by your own limited belief systems? Are you afraid to speak up for yourself? Do you give and give and then feel depleted? Do you take time to replenish yourself and fill yourself back up? Do you sometimes feel lost? Do you feel scared? Do you have feelings, emotions, fears and wounds swirling inside you that you don't know what to do with? Are you connected to yourself and to your inner power? Do you know how to be you? Do you know how to be the best version of you?

Most likely you are searching for a deeper fulfillment of life. Maybe you seek more self love, self acceptance and self reliance in your life. You might look to other people to give you love and affirmations, and determine your self worth or greatly influence it. Most likely you are plagued with wanting to please, be a good person and help others, usually at the cost of you. You have forgotten to take care of yourself. You have neglected yourself and stopped giving yourself recognition, acknowledgement, attention, adoration and self LOVE. Maybe you have been brainwashed to believe you are less than powerful, that your thoughts and feelings don't matter and that your voice is not worth listening to. You have tried to compete with the masses so you could stand out and be seen as special. You have forgotten your essence, your magic and your truth. You have forgotten how magnificent you are, how powerful you are and how much your influence can make this world a better place.

Your life matters. You are special. You are here to make some footprint. Perhaps to save the world, invent some new amazing product, raise healthy children, inspire others, be a star and shine in your own way. You are no accident. You are a miracle. Your life matters. There is only one unique you.

You are miraculous!

YOU ARE WORTHY!

I start here because you have most likely forgotten. At the core of your pain and suffering is you feel unworthy. Unworthy of love, money, success, bliss, beauty and ultimate health. You want to be seen, heard and loved. You want to feel you belong, you matter, you are accepted and your life is making a difference. You want everyone to see how good you are, how smart you are, how shiny you are because you are not seeing it in yourself first.

You are seeking out there. Out there love; Out there connection; Out there intimacy; Out there acceptance; Out there praise; Out there pats on the back and out there validation.

It's how we have been conditioned and taught in early days of school. An A+ or a D- to determine our self worth. Of course we all want it from our parents too, even when we are old and have kids of our own. We secretly crave the love, acceptance and pats on the back from our parents, telling us "YOU ARE A GOOD PERSON. I AM SO PROUD OF YOU. YOU ARE SO SMART. I TOTALLY SUPPORT YOU. YOU ARE WORTHY!"

Seeking, seeking, seeking self worth out there, when you can give it to yourself right now, right here, without anybody needing to be present.

You are like an electric chord trying to plug into other peoples' electrical sockets looking for validation and external energy to fill you up. When they give you energy, you are happy. When they don't give you energy, you are sad. Everyone out there has all the power and you need it to survive. To be truly powerful, you must learn to fill yourself up. You must learn to give yourself validation, acceptance, praise and adoring love.

This book can help. It is full of ideas, exercises and radical self reliance techniques to remind you of your greatness and your deeper internal power. It activates your inner excitement and passion for living and thriving on this planet. It expands your heart for those around you who truly matter, those you have most likely withheld yourself from. It teaches you to eat for optimal health, energy and vibrancy so you have a body you love and you don't get sick. It helps you create a stronger connection to your intuition and to your MAGNIFICENCE!

This book is a reminder of who you truly are and guides you to get back to your most magnificent self. It helps you reach inside and remember your fullest, greatest, happiest, most fully self expressed version of yourself. It will inspire and empower you. It is your personal mantra of empowerment as you read each and every word. The words will not only enter your brain, but will transform you on a physical cellular level as you rewire your mind to see your own greatness.

Most of us settle to live a mediocre version of ourselves and never express our full potential in this lifetime. We have not been taught that the thoughts we think and the words we speak ACTUALLY mold our reality. We have not been taught that we are powerful creators who can use mindfulness practices and empowering speech to create the life of our dreams.

Reading this book will help up level your experience of life.

Reading these powerful words, statements and perspectives will expand your responsibility to your life and to your reality. You will have a bigger understanding of your own power and of the miraculous human you are. This book is a personal mantra to yourself, so you can reprogram your mind for excellence and self mastery. With knowledge, inspiration and self mastery, you have a happier, more grounded experience of life.

BEAUTIFUL MAGICAL SOUL READING THIS, NOW IS YOUR TIME!

Are you struggling with self love, self acceptance, self worth, self discipline, self mastery and self connection?

Are you struggling with your health, body image, gut imbalances, inflammation, constipation and the confusion of what food to eat for optimal health?

Are you bickering over little insignificant things and avoiding deeper connection and intimacy?

Are your insecurities holding you back?

Now is your time to be more of who you want to be and to stop playing small. It is your time to shine your bright light and beautiful personality to the world, more confidently than you ever have before and to speak your deepest truth. If you have a deep throbbing desire TO DO SOMETHING, BE SOMETHING, BECOME SOMETHING, CREATE SOMETHING, then now is your time to do it.

I'm inviting you to jump on board of NO MORE excuses,

no more limitations, no more insecurities, no more diminishing your own light for fear of what others will think and no more you are not ready.

I'm inviting you to live your life even fuller, to shine your light even brighter, to sing your song even louder, to go after ALL your dreams with even more fervor, to lay in your grave knowing you played full out and rocked your life on your terms!

I'm inviting you to feel even more of your own power and magnificence, to look in the mirror and love who is looking back, to stop blaming everyone and everything out there for making you unhappy, to have more peace in your mind, to connect to your intuition stronger and to live your most extraordinary life ever!

You are on a journey, from birth to death you ride the waves of life. From the outside, your life is filled with dreams, goals, plans, movements and experiences. You might be disillusioned to believe that life is about the external gains you can see, touch and feel. Yet you are actually on an internal journey of self love, self acceptance, self worth, self mastery and self connection. As you master this internal journey, your external one becomes better and better. It is your time to master your internal journey.

Are you ready? Here we go! Grab my hand, I got you!
With Much Love & Aloha

Petra

CHAPTER 1

Time To I AM It!

I AM ARE THE 3 MOST POWERFUL LETTERS in your vocabulary. The words you put after them, shape your reality and determine what you declare about yourself. The words that come from your mouth are spells you weave. In every moment, you are creating your reality by the words you speak, the thoughts you think and the beliefs you have. What you believe about yourself IS your reality.

I am stupid. I am smart. You choose your reality by the power of these 3 letters. I know it sounds too simple. But it is. 3 letters can change your story, perception of life and reality. Most likely you speak your 'I AM' very unconsciously. You make a mistake and say, "I am stupid". You get stuck in a line and say, "I am unlucky". You don't have a date on Friday night and say, "I am not good enough". Without realizing it, you declare your reality and ask the universe to give more of it to you. What you declare will catch up to you, eventually become true and you will say, "I knew it. This always happens to me".

Learning to catch your 'I AM' as it flies out of your mouth is the first step to self mastery. Switching it to a much more empowering statement is the second step.

To help you MASTER your 'I AM', this book is written a little different. Instead of ME speaking to YOU, using the word YOU; I have written this book, as YOU speaking to YOU, using the words I AM. This book is your own personal mantra declaration of your life by using the words I AM to reprogram your mind and your reality.

Starting from this point, this book becomes your personal reprogramming as you read it. This is your I AM story and book. Word by word you will now be declaring your most inspired and empowered life. If you read it out loud, your declaration becomes even more powerful. If you use E.F.T (Emotional Freedom Tapping) while reading this book, your declaration becomes even more ingrained inside your whole being. This is an opportunity to experience this book as a personal transformation from within and witness the positive effects it has on you, instead of just reading it with your mind. This book is your new personal transformation tool.

This book is YOU reading this to YOU! I am no longer speaking to you as Petra, you are now reading this about yourself and reminding yourself of your own greatness, awareness, reality, power, knowledge and ability to create your life in any way that you desire. This is you talking to you....

I am reading this to myself now (me, the reader). This book has now become my tool of empowerment, inspiration, sovereignty, connection and self healing. I am perfect as I am in this moment. I read these words as an invitation to up level my health, my mind, my life and my self worth. I choose to remember what I may have forgotten. I choose to remember who I AM.

I REMEMBER MY
SUPER HUMAN POWERS
I TRAIN UP MY BODY, MY MIND AND MY HEART
TO BE EVEN MORE POWERFUL

THE WORLD NEEDS ME!
I NEED ME!
I'M GONNA ROCK THIS!

I AM AMAZING!
I AM ENOUGH
I AM ENOUGH
I AM ENOUGH

I declare the following to myself now...

I AM POWERFUL

I AM AMAZING

I AM STRONG

I AM BRAVE

I AM REALLY, REALLY SMART

I AM LOVEABLE

I AM SOOOOO LOVED

I AM LOVED BY THE UNIVERSE

I AM LOVED BY EVERYONE

I AM SPECIAL

I AM A SHINING BRIGHT LIGHT FOR SO MANY PEOPLE

I AM EXCEPTIONAL

I AM EXTRAORDINARY

I AM GOOD LOOKING, BEAUTIFUL, STUNNING

I AM CLEVER

I AM ENOUGH

I AM ENOUGH

CHAPTER 2

I Am Powerful

DECLARE THIS NOW BECAUSE IT IS the most important statement I (me, the reader) can speak. I (me, the reader) am powerful. Very, very, very Powerful. The more I believe that, feel that and live that knowing, the happier and more peaceful my life will be.

By powerful I don't mean world domination power. This power is different. It comes from the inside of me and it connects me to the infinite divine intelligent universe out there. This power is ME. Look at me, I am a miraculous amazing computer human being walking around the planet. Fully functioning to run, jump, chew gum, sing and solve mathematical equations at the same time. I am a coordinated, perfectly functioning, self healing organism on this planet. I am a miracle! A true miracle!

My body is an incredible machine that is always trying to heal me. In all moments, every second of the day. There is an innate self healing program inside my body that is running 24 hours a day, every day. I couldn't even stop this healing power if I wanted to. But why would I want to? My hair and fingernails, just keep growing. I don't have to do anything. It's automatic. My body is a computer machine and I am programmed for ultimate health, vitality and super human powers on this planet.

I am great. I am remembering my own greatness. I might have forgotten it. I might not have been told lately or I might have stopped believing in myself. I'm reminding me of my greatness. I have the ability to fine tune my body and my mind to create super feats and actions in my life. I, as a human, have so much potential to be anything and do anything that I chose. Once I set my mind to something, I can accomplish it. I am that powerful.

I am so impressive. I have the ability of consciousness, awareness and to be able to regenerate myself. My body is not solid or always the same. I am constantly regenerating. My cells are dying off and new cells are being regenerated. All in the background without me doing or knowing anything.

My skin replaces itself every 35 days. I am given a new liver every 6 weeks. My stomach lining replaces itself every 4 days and my stomach cells responsible for digesting my food replace every 5 minutes. My entire skeletal structure is replaced every 3 months. I have an entire new brain every 2 months. My entire super human body, right down to the last atom is replaced every 5-7 years.

Wow I AM IMPRESSIVE!

CHAPTER 3

I Am Great

KNOWING AND BELIEVING IN MY OWN GREATNESS is the foundation of my life. In order to have peace, love and happiness in my life, I must see myself as great. Amazing! Awesome! Spectacular!

I turn my energy in towards myself and see myself for real. Turn the camera, the lens, the attention right back on me and I reflect. How do I see myself? Awesome? Amazing? Ok? Good? Not Bad? Not really good enough? Not really worthy? A loser?

What are the words I am saying inside my head about myself? They are in there being said all the time. Am I really listening? I now listen with more awareness. I listen like I am an outsider eves dropping in on the conversation my inner voice is having with me ALL THE TIME.

What is it saying? "I am great! I am great! I am so proud

to be me! I am really cool. I totally dig me. I am so happy to be me". Or is it saying nasty stuff?

It takes awareness and practice. I can't change a habit if I don't know it exists. Mean self talk, diminishing myself, making myself small, beating myself up and punishing myself are OLD habits that I want to change. These are old ingrained patterns that I don't even know where I picked up. Perhaps my parents said diminishing things to me and I believed them, perhaps my bosses or teachers or partners told me I wasn't good enough, that I don't matter, that I am not loved and I believed them. Or perhaps no one told me I matter, that I am a worthy person on this planet and that I deserve this experience of life. Perhaps I wasn't told I was loved by my parents or told that they were proud of me or perhaps they didn't act like I really mattered or that my thoughts, feelings, beliefs mattered. Perhaps I believed all of it, all of them and I got pretty down about myself.

Up until now....

I am aware and ready for new perception shifts and transformations to see myself in even more glory. I love and appreciate myself. I am empowered. I create more love and healing in my life. I am great. I don't need anyone outside of me to tell me. I tell me. I am great and totally awesome. I spend time reflecting on my own greatness, on my value and on my amazingness. I am special. It's time for me to really know it and feel it inside my whole being. It's time for me to spend time with myself and reflect on my own greatness. I am great. So incredibly awesome and great! I know it! I feel it! I now live it with my whole being!

CHAPTER 4

I Am Enough

A S A KID, I CAME INTO THIS WORLD feeling enough, over flowing with joy and love. Yet at some point the feeling started to fade. My belief system of enoughness, self worth and self love got weaker. Somewhere along the way I got brainwashed to believe that I was not enough. Some incident in my life happened, that I believe was caused by my not enoughness. "If only I were enough my parents wouldn't divorce", "If only I were enough my partner wouldn't have left me", "If only I were enough my boss wouldn't have fired me". Maybe my enoughness was shoved out of me from a bully at school or an unaware teacher or my parents; Without even knowing it, something they said or did fed into my black hole of not enoughness and created a separation within me.

Somewhere I took on the belief that I am not enough. I am likely unaware of it. I likely never even thought of it before. I am likely going through my day, feeling what I am feeling, having my experiences and being in situations with people, feeling frustrated at life and myself, not realizing that my not enoughness is lurking in the dark at the root of it all.

I AM NOT enough is at the core of my suffering and my pain. This belief creates separation from myself, my loved ones and the universe. It wears many masks and has many layers so I have to dig deep if I want to uproot it. I am not alone. All humans in the world share the same internal pain. All of us have deep underlying beliefs that we are not enough, that we don't belong and that we are not worthy. Not enough is a low vibration experience. It is at the cause of my and everyone's depression, anxiety, stress, obesity, eating disorders, arguments, self hate, self sabotage, boredom, loneliness, illnesses and suicide.

If left on its own, this black hole of not enoughness will keep getting bigger and bigger and ruling more and more of my life. Time to stop!!! For myself and for humanity now! Reminding myself I am enough is so crucial. Reminding myself of my greatness and my abilities. Reminding myself of my gifts and my beauty. Always reminding myself first and then reminding others around me. I am enough. I do not have to do anything or be anyone to love myself. I love me. I am enough. I am perfect. I am enough and I support myself and love myself more and more. I raise my vibration with this simple new agreement I am making with myself starting right now "I AM ENOUGH"

In school I was NOT taught ENOUGHNESS TRAINING. So it's important that I talk about it now and learn how to feel enough at my core. It's important that I make the effort to uncover the source of my not enough belief system and rip it out at the root.

As a baby, I came into this life totally knowing I am enough. I saw no lack in myself. I saw myself as a perfect bundle of joy and love. People gushed all over me. Told me I am gorgeous. Adorable, Amazing, Miraculous, Smart and Marvelous. I gushed and ate it all up, giggled and was open for more and more. As an adult I have forgotten. I have forgotten my own greatness and my splendor. So instead of gushing when I am given a compliment, most of the time I deflect it, defend it and can't receive it because I don't believe it about myself. If I believe I'm not good enough then praise and appreciation will land on deaf ears.

This is Most Adults in conversation:

Person A - "You look so pretty today"
Person B - "Oh this old thing, I've had it forever and my hair looks terrible I need a hairdresser"

Person A - "You are so smart"
Person B - "Not really. I forget so much. I'm not as sharp as I used to be"

Person A - "I love you"
Person B – The internal subconscious voice says inside the person, "Well you wouldn't if you really knew me. At the core I'm unloveable, worthless and not enough. So how could you possibly love me? It's not real. Your love is not real. I don't love myself. So there is no way you can really love me." This

limiting language is spoken in the mind. The person is or isn't aware of this voice. Most likely it's in there deep and it lives at the root of it all.

This is Most Kids in conversation:

Kid A - "You are so smart and amazing"
Kid B - "Ya I know"

Kid A - "You are so powerful. You have super hero powers"
Kid B - "Ya I know. I can fly"

Kid A - "I love you"
Kid B - "Yes I love you too. I love you to the moon, infinity and this much as my arms can stretch out"

I AM enough and I AM NOT enough are belief systems. I get to chose what I want to believe. I am powerful. I am amazing! I am powerful enough to program my mind to believe what I want it to believe. I have a choice, I start right now. What am I going to choose? I am NOT enough or I AM ENOUGH!

Homework: Starting right now till the rest of my life.... repeat over and over in my head forever and forever till I die.....I AM ENOUGH - I AM ENOUGH - I AM ENOUGH

EXERCISE: RIPPING OUT MY NOT ENOUGHNESS AT THE ROOT

1. I close my eyes. I take a deep breath, hold it and now release it.

2. I do that a few more times till I feel lighter.

3. As I breathe in, I imagine grabbing all the garbage inside of me, all the stress, all the fights, all the frustrations, all the irritation and I let them go as I breathe out. I do this a few more times to lighten the load I carry inside of me.

4. I put my hand on the center of my heart. I keep my hand there. I keep breathing. I remember my own divinity.

5. I now breathe into the center of my heart. My big deep inhales lift my hand up and down and expand my chest wide.

6. I name a few things I am grateful for. I get connected to the vibration of gratitude and love in my heart.

7. I now ask myself, "Where did I first feel NOT ENOUGH? What is my earliest memory where I felt I am not enough?"

8. I stay here, breathing into my heart, lifting my hand up and down. My answer might take a few tries to come or I might get a flash of a memory or a thought. I don't dismiss it, think it's silly and move on. My intuition is strong.

9. If there is a memory, even if it feels silly. Then I go there, remember it and remember my feelings of not enoughness.

10. I now tell myself, "I AM ENOUGH" over and over again. "I AM ENOUGH.... I AM ENOUGH.... I AM ENOUGH.... I AM ENOUGH".

11. I tell myself, "This incident has nothing to do with my self worth. No one outside of me determines my self worth. I am enough. I am enough. I am a good person. I have always been enough. I love myself. I accept myself. I am enough".

12. I do the work on myself to reprogram my subconscious mind and sometimes I need a little help. Finding a subconscious programming practitioner could help me. I look into Theta Healing, EFT, Hypnosis, Repetition, Phych-K and Holosync to name a few.

CHAPTER 5

My Intuition

I HAVE AN INNER GUIDANCE SYSTEM THAT I AM born with. It is my internal compass that guides my path of life if I choose to listen. It can put me in all the right places, to meet all the right people and to help me create the life of my dreams. If I am not aware of this inner compass or am not listening to it, then my life will be more ungrounded, unsettled and unsure. Inside I have this feeling like I should be doing something different or that I should be somewhere different. Most likely my intuition is alerting me that I am not on purpose and it's giving me this weird gut feeling. This is why comments like, "I have a nagging feeling", "I felt that in my gut", "I had a gut feeling" are indicators that I am awakening to my inner voice, to my inner compass and am starting to listen to it.

My inner voice, my inner soul, my inner compass, my inner guidance system is speaking to me, directing my actions and leading me to fulfill my highest happiest purpose on this planet. It is my new best ally. It is my new best friend right by my side, to the end of my days. The one I can count on to steer me right. It's time to get to know this new best friend and connect to this being within me even deeper. Time to become best friends with myself. Time to listen. Truly listen to what my voice is speaking to me. So how do I hear it?

EXERCISE: CONNECTING TO MY INTUITION

1. I close my eyes and put my hand on my heart. I focus all my energy on my heart.

2. I breathe my hand up and down. I breathe into my heart.

3. I imagine a tree trunk and tree roots growing out of the base of my spine and rooting deep into the earth below me.

4. I am now centered in my body. I am now connected inside myself and I am grounded into the earth. I have pulled my energy in to myself. I am now inside my body.

5. Now I ask myself, "What do I want?", "What do I need?", "How can I be happier today?" and "How can I make my body healthier?" I listen. I keep asking. I keep listening. This is the path to my inner intuition, asking questions and listening to the answers that come from within me. My internal voice will get stronger and I will get better at hearing it as I practice over and over again.

CHAPTER 6

In My Body

OST OF THE TIME I AM NOT LIVING in my body. I place my energy (which is my life force, my thoughts and emotions) into the past or the future. In the past, I am thinking about the fight I had with my spouse a few days ago or clinging to the younger version of myself from the past. In the future, I am already living in my upcoming vacation and imagining myself already there or I am letting my fantasy run wild imagining the life I will have with the new lover I just met.

I am rarely living in the present moment. I am rarely fully present inside my body. Especially if I had any body trauma in the past or bad body image or sexual abuse, then living and being inside my body is not comfortable or fun. So I would rather focus my energy somewhere else, instead of in my body which I associate so much pain with. So I live out there.

But why is it important to be inside my body? Well, because my body is speaking to me in all moments. It is directing me with little aches and pains. It is directing me with signals.

My intuition which lives in my body, is speaking to me and is directing my life and my choices. If I am not home to listen, then all this universal divine intelligence information passes me by.

My body knows which healing foods it really wants to eat and if I start listening I can feed my body for optimal nutrition. I can use my body intuition to help make healthier food choices and direct me in the right way. I will not be asking my body if it wants chips, pop or a hotdog and then listening for the answer. No! The body really wants neither choice, it's my mind and taste buds that have trained me to like the chemical, sugary unhealthy foods. My body only wants the good stuff and once it gets healthier it will tell me when it wants something green or something fatty or needs more protein.

My body is also giving me signals of pain and discomfort. If I listen, I can catch sickness or illness at a very early stage and do something about it. Or I can continue to ignore my body's signals and the signals will get louder and the sickness worse. My body is always working for my greatest healing and thriving. It gives me signals as warning signs that my body is starting to malfunction.

If was driving my car and the oil indicator started blinking I would not put a piece of tape over the blinking light and keep driving. No, because eventually my car would break down. It's the same with my body. If I don't listen to the signals, eventually my body will break down. From now on, I take care of my body like I would take care of my automobile. I give it tune ups, change the oil, clean it, give it the best fuel and take care of any problems it has. My body engine loves me.

Sometimes I abuse my body with alcohol, toxic food, cigarettes, stress, harsh thoughts and drugs. I withhold nutrients, vitamins, juicy raw fruits, vegetables, water, smoothies and juices from myself. I feed myself junk food garbage instead of healthy food, as a strange form of punishment, lack of connection and lack of self love for myself. I change that. I listen to my body, which LOVES me and is helping me. I give my body self love, self care and self nurturance on a daily basis.

I am aware that my body cannot run forever without me taking the time to care for it. Years and years of abuse will eventually catch up to me. Why wait till I get sick or too fatigued before I do something? It is time for me to care for my health now before a sickness forces me to HAVE TO do it. As I create a friendship with myself and a better relationship with my body, I will think twice before I feed it crap. This friendship might take a while to develop, yet soon I will worship my body as the sacred temple and miraculous machine that it is.

I love my body and I love my life. As I love my body, I have more peace within myself. I accept myself and accept how I have been created. I appreciate all my curves, bumps and fingernails. I feel content when I look in the mirror. I am my own best friend. I am my greatest admirer. I accept my body as the greatest gift, the universal intelligence could have given me. This body of mine is miraculous. It is a walking and living miracle. I stop and focus on the miracle of me. I drop into the gratitude of my body and all it does for me. I apologize for all the abuse I have given my body and I promise to take better care of it from now on. I worship myself and my sacred body temple. I am made up of so many moving parts, so many little pieces, so much energy, so much water, so much blood, so much magic and I am in awe of myself. I wake up every morning and give thanks for this spectacular body, functioning for me just another day. I give thanks to the universal intelligence for breathing me yet another day. At the end of my day I give thanks to be alive and I give thanks to be the amazing incredible beautiful spectacular miraculous juicy extraordinary ME!!!

EXERCISE: CONNECTING TO MY BODY

1. I breathe into my heart. I breathe into my body. I feel the breath in my body.

2. I feel my belly moving up and down. I feel my chest moving up and down.

3. I put my hands on my body. I touch my body. I pat my body. I feel my hands touching my body.

4. I am now connected to my body.

5. I ask my body, "What do you need?", "Where is the pain?", "Where is the blocked energy?", "What part of you wants my attention right now?". And I listen. I might not hear anything right away. So I keep asking and keep listening as my connection to myself gets stronger.

I AM ENOUGH

I AM ENOUGH

I AM ENOUGH

I EXIST

I AM A SPARK OF LIFE

I AM CREATION

I BREATHE

LIFE BREATHES ME

I AM ENOUGH

...

I DON'T NEED TO DO ANYTHING TO EARN LOVE
I AM LOVED BECAUSE I AM BORN
LIFE LOVES ME, LIFE GAVE ME LIFE
THE UNIVERSE LOVES ME
THE UNIVERSE IS ON MY SIDE AND HAS MY BACK
I AM ENOUGH
I DON'T NEED ANYONE TO TELL ME
I AM ENOUGH, I KNOW IT
I AM GOOD ENOUGH, I AM GOOD ENOUGH
I AM GOOD, I AM REALLY REALLY GOOD
I AM A GREAT PERSON, I AM A REALLY GOOD PERSON
I AM LOVED
I AM ENOUGH, I AM ENOUGH
I AM FORGIVEN, I FORGIVE MYSELF
I AM WORTHY
I AM WORTHY OF LOVE, KINDNESS AND PEACE
I DESERVE IT, IT IS MY BIRTHRIGHT
I AM ENOUGH

CHAPTER 7

Mirror, Mirror

W HAT HAPPENS WHEN I LOOK IN THE MIRROR? Do I feel love or self loathing? Do I say nice things or nasty things to myself? Do I smile at the being looking back at me or scowl and frown? Do I see beauty or lines, wrinkles and bags under my eyes? What happens and what is said inside my head? What are the thoughts, the words and the feelings when I look at myself in the mirror? Do I love and adore myself?

This face is it. Unless I use plastic surgery on myself, this face, these eyes, this mouth, this nose is what will always look back at me. I love it. I see my own beauty. I love me. I honor me. I appreciate me.

Can I really start loving myself by looking in the mirror? Currently when I look in the mirror, I don't feel really great things about myself. I feel anger, sadness and despair. I see all the imperfections and maybe I fear facing my own eyes in the mirror. I fear connection to myself. I fear being real and I fear being truthful with myself. I've been running away from myself far too long. Even if I haven't realized it, I've made other people's opinions and advice way more important. Rather than tuning in to my own intuition and asking what I really thought and wanted, I've asked other people.

I've searched far too long for external validation. External decision making for my life choices from strangers who knew not what was truly in my heart. I've asked friends if I should stay in a relationship or break up? I've asked other people what I want to wear or what I want buy? When all along my intuition knew best.

I've used the mirror as a form of punishment to myself and sometimes would rather not look at my own reflection. I might look when I feel fresh, done up or dressed up but avoid the mirror when I am feeling low or emotional. I try on clothes but use the mirror to judge and scold my own body and brew deeper in the vibrations of not enoughness, self doubt and self loathing.

Well it's time to stop all this nonsense isn't it? Time to laugh off my limitations and step into a bigger version of myself. My playing small is not serving the world so it's time to start in the most important place ever, it's time to LOVE AND ADORE MYSELF! The fastest way I know how to start loving and adoring myself, to start seeing my entire world shift, to morph and transform for the BETTER is to use a mirror.

"Mirror, Mirror on the wall – who is the fairest of them all?"

The best part is – I get to choose my answer to that question. No magical mirror genie has power of me, I get to choose myself as the fairest of them all and love myself as my most favorite person on the planet.

My intention for myself starting right now, is to start brewing more thoughts of self adoration and self love. I say more kind encouraging words to myself. I reflect on my words and actions with wonder instead of judgment. I question how I show up in the world so I can always show up better. I open my heart more and more. I love who is staring back at me in the mirror. I have the confidence and assurance that I am enough and I am amazing.

So I start loving myself right now, right here with a mirror...

EXERCISE: CREATING MORE SELF LOVE

1. I look at myself in the mirror. (Smart phone selfie camera works as option #2 if a mirror is not around)

2. I notice the self talk. I breathe.

3. I keep looking into my eyes. I keep breathing.

4. I look into one eye, then the other eye, then both eyes at the same time. I can't do this wrong. This is my own connecting journey.

5. I say out loud, "I love you" "I really love you_____(fill in my name)".

6. I keep saying these two sentences over and over.

7. I add, "I'm proud of you. You are amazing. I am happy to be you. I got you. You are safe. I am here to take care of you. I love you".

8. I listen as my intuition bubbles up and tells me what else to say. I listen and say it out loud to myself. No one is around. No one is watching. No one cares. This is my personal journey with myself. This is my personal get to know myself and fall in love with myself journey.

9. What do I want to say to myself? What conversation do I want to have? Do I want to forgive myself? Praise myself? Acknowledge myself? Get real with myself? Get truthful with myself?

10. I do this mirror exercise daily. Maybe even a few times a day. Every morning or every evening. I do it often. I don't stop doing it for the rest of my life. I keep connecting with myself and building my relationship with the most important person on the planet. ME!

CHAPTER 8

My Inner Child

I AM GOING TO TAKE ON THE IDEA that there is a little being living inside of me, approximately a 7 year old little mini me that won't ever grow up. Quietly it obeys all my commands or at times resists me with a torrential tantrum. This little being inside, despite me being 'all grown up', still wants to be seen, heard, held, nurtured, hugged, kissed and adored just like when I was a child.

This inner child feels the fears, neglects, rejections, doubts, insecurities and is looking to my adult self for connection and assurance that everything is going to be ok.

Most likely, I have neglected myself. Neglected my needs, my wants, my desires, my visions and my inner child is PISSED OFF!

That inner peace I seek cannot be achieved if my inner child is upset and throwing tantrums of anger, jealousy, neglect and rage. The fastest way to my inner peace is to connect with my inner child and soothe its soul.

I think as a kid, I was very connected to my inner child. I WAS this inner child. I was congruent. I said what I felt. I did what I wanted. I pushed rules to see my boundaries. I was alive, present, alert, completely heart centered and connected to myself and the universe all around me. (Unless I was numbed with TV and video games which took away my child's alert presence).

Somewhere along the path I got further and further disconnected from my inner self, my inner child, my inner intuition and my inner soul. I got focused on grades, studying, job interviews, work politics, children, family, dating, marriage, stress, not fitting into my jeans and eventually just feeling overwhelmed by it all. So connecting to my inner child and listening to what it had to say, well that was just another thing on my plate that I couldn't handle.

Well guess what? I can handle it and I got this and it's time to rock out my life, be inspired and in love with myself. It's time to stop neglecting myself and time to start asking and listening to my inner child and giving it what it needs.

It's time to take my inner child out on dates, buy it healthy nourishing amazing food, put it into only positive high vibrational places and surround it with only kind considerate and compassionate people. It's time to give my inner child so much love, acceptance and appreciation. Yes! It's time I GIVE THIS TO ME NOW!

No one else can fill my void! Only I can! It starts with my inner child.

For too long I have searched for validation, safety, acceptance, appreciation, acknowledgement, self worth and love out there. I energetically reached out my tentacles to everyone else to fill me in some way. To remind me of what I have forgotten to accept as my birthright – that I AM MIRACULOUS AND DIVINE!

So I kept asking out there, "What should I do?", "Where should I go?", "Who should I be with?", "What should I eat?", "What should I wear?" and "What should I say?" Walking around miserable, disconnected, ungrounded and in a state of insecurity. I have been self loathing myself with indecision hoping someone out there has the answers and validation, I so desperately seek.

Maybe I marry because I want to feel self worth. Maybe I stay in relationships too long because I am not listening to my intuition. Maybe I don't pursue my dreams because I am too afraid of what everyone else will think and say. I walk around in a state of paranoia and craziness, saying unkind words quietly inside my head, feeling grateful that no one can actually hear my internal nasty voice. At times I feel I am slowly going crazy and it seems there is no way out of the rat race.

But there is – it's my internal work. I create my body and my mind to be healthy, peaceful and vibrating at a high frequency. I create myself from the inside out because every thing I see and feel outside of myself has been projected from inside of me. It's my movie. It's my dream. I am the projector and I choose the type of movie I play. So cleaning up the inside muck, taking control of the projector and owning my reality 100% is the key to living my most extraordinary life.

So I clean up the muck by first cleaning up the relationship I have with myself. I clean up my relationship with my inner child. Have I said sorry to myself lately? Appreciated myself? Told myself I am proud of me? Have I forgiven myself for my wrongs and have I let them all go?

The relationship I have with this inner being is just like any external relationship I have. In order for it to thrive, I need to clean up the old muck. Say sorry. Forgive. Let go. Be heard. Listen. Cry. Acknowledge and become more connected to myself. I have to wrap my arms around myself and give myself a big squeeze! Right now!

So I must go through this ritual with myself. I have to finally see myself. Look at all my wrongs and forgive. I have to see me.

I can't keep looking out there for others to see me. I have to see me.

I can't keep looking out there for others to appreciate me and tell me I matter. I have to tell me.

I can't keep looking out there for others to validate me and acknowledge my existence. I have to do this.

My life is in my hands. I am in charge. I own my life

creation and my life journey. I stop being a victim. No one is coming to save me. I have to save me. I have to own this life of mine, hop in the driver's seat and go smash out my goals and my dreams. Only I can do this. No one else is coming!

EXERCISE: CONNECTING TO MY INNER CHILD

1. I wake up in the morning and just lie there. I don't engage with anyone. Not even my dog.

2. I stay solitary with myself.

3. I keep my eyes closed. I breathe.

4. I put my hand on my heart.

5. I think of my inner child. My 7 year old being living energetically inside me. Does it have a name? Listen an answer may come. I name my inner child right now. Some mini version of myself.

6. I connect to this being.

7. I say, "good morning_____(your inner child name)... I love you".

8. I ask, "what is it you need today?" "What will make you happy today?"

9. I listen to my inner child for the answer.

10. I take time to ask again or a few times if I can't hear the answer at first. Maybe it takes a few days to hear the answer. Maybe my child has been silent for so long that it is too shy to speak up.

11. I am patient. I give love and acceptance to myself during this new dialogue communication. I am not mad at myself or think I'm stupid, if I can't hear the answer right away. It takes practice. I am patient. I am kind to myself.

I LOVE MYSELF

CHAPTER 9

I Am Energy

I AM AN ENERGETIC BEING. I AM MADE UP of energy. My body is made up of atoms that are continuously giving off and absorbing light and energy all the time. It doesn't even stop when I sleep. My body keeps radiating light and energy. Every cell in my body is lined up in such a way that it has a negative and positive voltage. Every one of my cells is a miniature battery. Each cell has 1.4 volts of energy, multiplied by 50 trillion cells in my body, that's a voltage of 700 trillion volts of electricity running through my body. Wow my body is so powerful and I am so powerful if I know how to use this energy. This energy is called chi and I have it inside me. Every living thing has chi.

I am sure I have felt this chi energy before. I am sure I have felt energy inside my body. For example, when I stand up and get dizzy, I can feel the energy swirling around in my head. Or I walk into a room and can feel the tension or energy in there. After vigorous exercise or wild love making, I can feel the energy coursing through my body. This is my chi energy or also called my Kundalini energy. There is plenty of scientific proof that I am made up of energy. I can do more research if I am curious and will uncover many wondrous things. So why is this important? Because I can change my energy depending on what ever frequency I tune to. I can tune to any radio frequency of energy and I get to choose.

Telling myself, "I am powerful, I am amazing, I am worthy" tunes me to a higher vibration then words like "I suck, I am stupid, I am a loser". So I get to choose what vibration I want to tune to and what vibration I want to help others tune to. Telling someone, "You are stupid. You are bad. You never listen. You are a loser" will program them for failure and self hate. My words have energy and vibration too, so I speak my words consciously to everyone around me. My words and my thoughts have power. I use my power for good, not for evil.

The power of me being energetic, means I can self heal too. Disease in the body is just a dis-ease of energy flow. Somewhere something is stuck, blocked and energy cannot flow. So by using holistic practices to move, cleanse and clean my body's energy, I can self heal myself from even the worst diseases. I remember my body is a self healing machine. It is healing me in all moments. The more help I can give my body, the better and faster my transformation happens.

CHAPTER 10

Vibration Scale

A N AWESOME BOOK TO READ ON THIS TOPIC and so much more is David Hawkins "Power Vs Force". In the book he has a vibration scale of words and emotions and where they rate in frequency. His work is done through kinesiology, muscle testing and tapping into the body's own innate intuitive power.

Shame, guilt, anger, hate, rate very low on the vibration scale. Where as emotions like peace, love and joy rate much higher up the scale. The higher up the scale my body emotion is, the happier, healthier and freer I will feel.

So it's up to me to climb the ladder of vibration as much as possible and keep expanding and opening up my own vibration. The more I can let myself be in joy, gratitude, self love, peace and appreciation, the more I can raise my own vibration. The more I hang out with kids, who are oozing with joy and vibration, the more I can let it wash over me, fill every cell of my being and raise my own vibration.

My words have vibrations. My thoughts have vibrations. My experiences have vibrations. My relationships have vibrations. My actions have vibrations. Moving up the scale of vibration and being fully aware it exists is a daily awareness I must master to be a super human on this planet. Constantly choosing high vibration uplifting thoughts WILL raise my vibration, eating healthy life giving food WILL raise my vibration, surrounding myself with amazing people WILL raise my vibration and putting myself into positive beautiful heart centered environments WILL raise my vibration. My words and thoughts can create love, intimacy and connection or they can create war, separation and pain. My thoughts have vibrations and can be felt by others, even if I never speak them out loud. Yes people can sense my energy, my thoughts and my intentions on a telepathic energetic level.

This is important to understand, **we can sense each other's energy and thoughts without them ever being spoken.** The person beside me might not know the words I am saying inside my head, but they can certainly feel the energy and vibration of the thoughts I am having. I'm sure I've had experiences where I said something quite innocent to a friend but they sensed some tone in there and felt hurt. If I focus on defending what I said, I will be justified as the words I used were authentic. Yet if I really look inside myself a little deeper, I might see that I was feeling annoyed on the inside trying to suppress these feelings and so my tone came out in a vibration that my friend sensed and got hurt by.

I know it. I know this energy thing is real. I can feel it. I have felt it. I have felt this tingling feeling of something's wrong before. Or this feeling like something is about to happen. Or I've sensed people's energy without them saying anything.

It is crucial to be aware of the thoughts I think about someone sitting beside me. These thoughts that I think are so secretly hidden, I am now aware are actually affecting others by the vibration they hold. I now use the power of my words and my thoughts more intentionally and create more positive high vibration energy in the world with my power.

The cool thing is that each person on the planet vibrates at a certain frequency. So when I meet someone, I either feel 'good vibes' or 'bad vibes', depending on if our frequency waves are in synch. That is how I can be magnetically attracted to someone or repelled by them. My energy is always mixing with the energy of people all around me. We are all interconnected and affected by each other's energies. It is important for me to stay aware of the people and environments I get entangled in. Are they constructive energy waves or destructive ones?

My body knows instinctively what environments, situations and people are nourishing and which are toxic. All animals on the planet communicate through vibrations, sensing whether energy is good for them or not. I have not been trained as a human to use these super powers of instinct, so I must learn to use them now. I stop listening to what people are saying. I stop asking people for opinions about my life. I stop. I breathe. I touch my body. I connect to my body. I listen to my inner voice. I listen to my intuition. I listen to my inner guidance system. I listen to my body's wisdom and see what it has to say. I meditate and tune in to myself. I tune in to check if I am surrounded by positive high vibrations or low negative low ones.

I adjust my vibration and raise my vibration when ever possible. I work on climbing up the vibration scale in the way I live my daily life. I bring more love, gratitude, peace, justice and kindness to all those around me. I think happier thoughts. I love myself more.

I feed myself high vibration raw living life force food, smoothies and juices. I look in the mirror and love who is looking back. I heal all the places in my life that hold a low vibration. I forgive people. I move on. I let go. I purge. I cleanse out the old so I have space for the new. I put myself into situations that feed my soul and bring me to life. I surround myself with people who love me, appreciate me and respect me. I lift myself higher and higher. I bring more and more light into my life and add in more and more happy every day. I reach for higher vibrating thoughts and think about the words I use. I pull myself out of the dark. I bring myself into the light. I can do this. Only I can. Only I can vibrate myself higher with the power of my mind and how I clean and fuel my body temple. I am in charge. Yes I am powerful! I am amazing! I love myself!

"Everything is energy and that's all there is to it. Match the frequency of the reality you want and you cannot help but get that reality. It can be no other way. This is not philosophy. This is physics."
– *Albert Einstein*

CHAPTER 11

I Speak My Truth

O NE OF THE GREATEST GIFTS AND POWERS I have is the ability and freedom to speak my truth. It might be easy for me or it might be the most painful difficult thing to do. Why is speaking my truth so difficult and painful?

Firstly I am most likely not connected to my truth. I am not connected and listening to my wise deep all knowing intuition. Or I hear something speaking within me and I disregard it as nonsense or silliness and move on. Secondly I am most likely afraid to speak my truth. I am afraid to not be understood, not be heard, perhaps be laughed at, ostracized and fearful love will leave me.

The crazy, amazing, bizarre, unforeseen thing that happens though is that every time I hold back speaking my truth for fear of hurting others or myself, my lack of truth creates more pain, chaos and hurt for both parties involved. The lack of being internally congruent within myself will show up as dragons breathing fire in other places. Becoming brave, loving myself enough and grounding into myself will allow me to speak my truth to another with peace, grace and ease.

I fear love leaving me. I fear not being accepted. I fear being shamed. I hold all my truth inside as it brews and bubbles ready to burst out. My deep inner unspoken truths wreak havoc on all my organs, my body, my mind and my heart. I can't be fully present and alive in my life if I am holding back speaking my truth. I refuse to pretend anymore or live a façade and choose to experience the depth of authenticity that I truly desire and deserve.

Sometimes my truth comes out in rage. Sometimes I even 'cause fights' so I can finally release all the bottled up truths I have been feeling and not sharing. I scream in the 'game of anger' feeling like I finally have the freedom to speak my truth and now I don't even have to sugar coat it, I can let it out fully. I let the other person have it, puke all my deep suppressed truths I have been afraid to share, all over them. If I am afraid to speak my truth, for fear that love will leave me, then these suppressed emotions will eventually come out in anger. The cruel words I speak could very well ensure that love leaves me. The thing I feared most.

Sometimes I won't lash out at someone with my truths but I will lash in. I will self hate myself with cigarettes, alcohol, unhealthy food, lack of sleep, nasty self talk and constant verbal poison. I will put myself into situations and relationships that are not healthy for me. I believe I don't deserve better or am afraid to speak up for myself, so I torture myself with fear and paralyzation.

So how do I speak my truth and why is it important?

It's important because it's my life. It's my authenticity. It's my heart's longing and deepest soul feelings that want to be shared. I deserve to be heard, seen and gotten. I cannot live a dualistic fake life and expect to feel vibrant and healthy. Health and wellbeing come from the inside. I can only feel peaceful with myself, when I speak up for myself, when I speak up for my rights, when I share my feelings, when I express myself, when I honor my own truth and speak it.

My truth is my truth. I trust it. I honor me. I believe in me and I believe in what my intuition is telling me. I listen. I trust. I listen. I trust. I listen. I trust.

When my truth comes from my heart, it is delivered to another's heart. When my truth comes from my head, it is delivered to another's head. I can chose to have a heart to heart conversation with someone or a head to head conversation. When my truth comes from my heart, there is a vibration behind it that has resonance and rings with truth. Maybe the other will get upset, not like what I am saying, scream, leave the room or leave my life yet I know that if I speak my truth, speak from my heart, take ownership of my life and my reality then I cannot control another's experience or response. I may not like losing a friend or making someone cry, yet I can feel proud for speaking what is real for me and knowing that in the end it is for the highest good of us all.

Speaking my truth is my evolution of self love for myself. Being in integrity with my thoughts, my words and my soul's longing creates peace and connection in my body and to the bigger picture of this universe. I feel stronger. I feel more in my power. I feel more alive. I feel more in control of my life and my destiny. I practice speaking my truth often, until speaking my truth is a normal way of being for me and becomes second nature, just like breathing. I love and honor myself, I speak up for what my heart and soul desire and for what they communicate to me. I listen to my intuition. I realize what is right for me. I speak my truth with love and kindness.

If I have children, then teaching them to speak their truth is crucial to their freedom and personal development as sovereign beings on this planet. Most children do not speak their truth to their parents for fear of the consequences, so they hold all their thoughts and emotions inside. Once enough stuff builds up on the inside, kids start talking back, disrespecting their parents and perhaps the terrible teens become extra explosive.

As a parent, I am the space for my children to speak their truth freely without fear of being in trouble or my love leaving them. I allow my children a safe space to speak what is inside their heart, what hurts them, what bothers them, what they desire, what they need and this creates a nurturing safe relationship between us. I give my children the experience, that what they say and feel is important. My children feel safe to share with me and they trust me to be there for them and to listen to them.

Maybe it's easy for my children to speak their truth when it comes to what they want for lunch, how a kid treated them at school or how much they love me. I might think we have a close relationship because they tell me stuff. But I am curious, do they feel safe enough to tell me really personal stuff and stuff about me? About the rules I set for them? About the soccer practice or ballet lessons I push them into weekly? Are they too afraid to disappoint or upset me, so they stay quiet? Is it safe for them to speak to me about ANYTHING? If my children stay 'quiet', then eventually this bottled up emotion will start showing up in different ways. Perhaps they will start talking back, stop listening to me, stop respecting me and eventually start creating trouble to be noticed and to express the frustration they feel on the inside.

So I treat my children with respect, listen to their heart's voice and give them space to safely speak their truth. They will trust me and we will create a much deeper bond and relationship. My children will 'let me in' more in to their inner world and the feelings they are having. This will help me support, guide and nurture them on a whole new level. When I know what lights up their heart and what their inner voice is saying, I can support them better.

EXERCISE: SPEAKING MY TRUTH TIPS
FOR ADULTS AND CHILDREN

1. No matter what age I am, starting to speak my truth and use this muscle can be difficult.

2. I practice slowly and confidently speaking my truth on a daily basis. Slowly because at first, it might feel like a volcano erupting. I will have a comment, opinion and truth for everyone. I might feel so blocked up for years that once I open the flood gates, I can't stop. My truth might not come out gently and kindly. So I go slowly. I think of the words I am using. I speak from my perspective. I speak from what I am feeling. No one did anything to me or made me feel a certain way. I am in charge of how I feel and I get to choose if someone upsets me or not. I am kind. The kinder I tell my truth, the more likely I will be met with kindness back. If I speak with hostility, anger and blame, I might get the same coming back at me. "You did this and you made me feel stupid", changes to "you did this and I experienced feeling stupid". No one can make me feel anything. I am not a victim and they are not the aggressor. I trust that everyone is innocent and everything is a misunderstanding at best. Their behavior just triggered something inside of me and it hurt. I am in control of that trigger and if I let my wound of feeling stupid affect me, then that is my choice.

3. I learn what my truths are. I tune into myself. I meditate. I connect to my heart. I breathe into my heart. I ask myself, "what do I want? What will make me happy? What does my heart and soul need right now? Is this right for me?"

I listen. My answers might not come right away. But eventually they will come.

4. I practice with my partner, friend or family. "I'm learning to really speak my truth right now and so I want your patience. I want you to listen to me, to hear me and to receive me with as much love as possible. I want you to accept this new part of myself for our relationship and for the deeper relationship I am creating with myself right now."

5. I give my self love, adoration, encouragement, support, respect and safety to speak my truth. Just as I would encourage a child, I encourage and love myself in this same way.

6. Speaking my truth will create more joy, love, trust and connection. People might not like what I have to say, but if it is my truth, then they will respect me.

7. If I want others to hear my truth, then I also have to be a safe place for other people to share their truth with me. I can't just expect people to share stuff with me, if I am not a safe space to receive their stuff. I might think I am a great listener or great confidant but if my energy closes once the person starts speaking, then I am not a safe space for someone to share their truth with me.

8. A safe space is an open heart. An open mind. An open energy. It is not taking anything personal and instead allowing the person speaking to have their experience, feelings and emotions. It is being compassionate, kind, loving and nurturing. It is being a safe space to have someone tell me their heart's

secrets. Listening is an art. The alternative is judging, reacting, deflecting, changing the subject, belittling or squishing the other person's energy. I am not committed to that.

9. Speaking my truth is an art too. It is a muscle I practice so that I learn to speak in a kind, truthful and heart centered way. I practice so my message is heard in the heart and received in love, instead of starting a war. All too often when I am scared to speak my truth, the energy bottles up and erupts out of me as I get mad. I start screaming all my internal truthful statements that are dripping with anger, resentment and hate and thinking I am finally speaking my truth. Puking all my frustration and hate on someone is not speaking my truth with love. This way will leave me and the other person feeling terrible and I am not committed to that.

CHAPTER 12

This Is My Reality

W HAT IF I TOOK ON THE MOST RADICAL concept of this entire book. It might stretch me to think this way or it might seem incomprehensible. I might think it's woo woo or out there thinking. I might be so caught in my story of victim consciousness that this form of empowerment might seem unrealistic. But hey I wake up! I am that powerful! So I open my mind to take on this new concept and try it out. What have I got to lose but another year of my life not being as amazing and living another year of mediocrity. No thanks!

Ok here goes.

This life of mine is 100% my responsibility. I get to choose how I feel and react in any situation. I get to see the world as a good place or a bad place. I get to shut off the valve of love from flowing or I get to open it. I have the power to apologize and make any situation right. I can forgive. I can change my story. I can change my mind. I don't have to take it personally.

I don't have to let anything or anyone effect me. I am powerful. This life is my creation.

I am a movie projector and my movie is projected on the external screen of my life. I think it's happening to me, yet in fact I am pulling it all in with my vibration and belief system. Changing my vibration, changes my belief system and changes my life. It's actually that easy. When I can fully let go of victim consciousness, and I mean fully let go, then a new form of power sets in, a personal power that no one can take away from me. It's a personal power that is my greatest asset on this planet. Once I really understand that I am 100% responsible and fully in charge of how my life is turning out, then I can finally do something about it instead of waiting for someone to come do it for me. Instead of looking to others for stuff to change, I am in charge to do this for myself.

I keep looking at my internal movie projector and asking... "Why am I creating this? Why am I attracting this into my life? What do I believe about myself? What limiting thoughts do I have? Where can I up my game? Where can I shift my thinking? Where can I open up? Who can I forgive? What can I let go of? What is this showing me? How can I create a new possibility and a new outcome?"

Movies like the Matrix and Avatar give me a glimpse into this idea that perhaps I am dreaming up my life right now and it's time for me to awaken within my dream and start creating my life with intention rather than from reaction. In these movies the characters can awaken within their dream and recognize that they are dreaming it all up. So now I imagine I can too....

I am dreaming it all up. My external world is a holographic projection of my internal movie. I have come to this planet and put myself into my body skin bag machine to carry me around and allow me to live my existence on this planet as a human. I am energy. I fill my body skin bag with energy that makes me move, think, walk, talk and cry. I am powerful. I am energy. I am light. I am connected to everything because everything is me. Everything is energy too. Some energy is moving very quickly so it's thinner, more transparent and more pliable like water and hopefully my body. Other energy is moving much slower so it's dense and cannot be altered easily like a rock or a wood stump and sometimes my body.

I can choose my vibration and I can choose my reality. I can vibrate higher and have a lighter, more illuminated experience of life. I can vibrate lower and a have a denser, darker, heavier experience of life.

I get to choose.

There are ways I can raise my vibration and vibrate much higher. The tools and teachings in this book help me vibrate much higher, help me illuminate, shine more light and elevate my own soul and consciousness. I've heard of enlightenment but didn't know how to achieve it. I assumed being enlightened was saved for monks in caves or all day meditators. Enlightenment is actually totally doable for me to achieve.

To be enlightened, I must lighten and invite more light into my body and mind. By lightening my own energy and energetic field I will be enlightening myself. The fastest way to enlighten my energy is to cleanse my body and get rid of all the excess built up chemicals, environmental pollutants, preservatives, toxic food, excess fecal matter, dirty cells and dirty blood. Also cleanse my body of toxic thoughts, toxic relationships, toxic self loathing, toxic resentment and toxic stress.

Then I must rebuild my body with light elevating raw food, smoothies, juices, spring water and super foods. Instantly my body will vibrate at a much higher frequency. I will have more energy. I will feel more awake. My issues will come up to the surface to be healed. **Heavy food and chemicals will keep my issues buried in my tissues, poisoning me daily.** So when I stop stuffing my issues down with heavy food, mind numbing TV and toxic habits, they will rise to the surface and show their not so pretty heads. It's my job to kiss the issues, love them, see them, heal them, acknowledge them, transmute them and say good bye to them, forever!

I lighten my thoughts, my beliefs, my judgments, my resentments, my body skin bag, my heart, my soul, my story, my fears and my beliefs. I lighten the energy I have all around me. I lighten up my environments, my home, my car, my office. I lighten up my judgments I carry over people and I release them to be free. I lighten up my house, I open up the windows and let the fresh purifying air in. I remove everything blocking light from coming into my house. I open blinds and remove all that blocks bright light from entering into my life. I invite in more light and more levity. The more I eat light, the more I will levitate.

I lighten up my body and become more bendable. I am more flexible with my movements and with my thoughts. I am pliable. I am open. I always learning, changing, shifting and transforming. I am not afraid of change. I may be uncomfortable with it and it may take me some time to get used to, but I am open to transformation. I go with the flow of the earth and nature that is always changing and transforming. The weather patterns change and flow from one day to the next. There is nothing to fear, just a different weather day. The seasons change, the trees change, the flowers change, the grass changes and I change. I keep my body loose and pliable like a green leaf falling from a tree. Juicy, green, bendable and alive with freshness. What is my alternative? An old dried up leaf that if stepped on will crack, break and shatter. I let go of fixed cemented concrete firm dense thinking and lighten up.

I lighten up who I am; My personality, my beliefs and dogmatic only-my-way-or-the-highway-have-be-right attitude. I create more space within. The more space I create, the more space there is for the NEW to come in. New opportunities. New friendships. New relationships. New ideas. New creations. I start looking deeper at how I show up in the world? What is the energy I put out there? How does my energy interact with other people's energy in the world? How do I leave people feeling? Do I leave a positive footprint on people I interact with? Do I leave them feeling uplifted or do I drop their vibration?

How do I impact others? My spouse? My partner? My ex? My kids? My friends? My gas attendant? My teacher? My coworker? My cell phone customer service agent? The homeless person on the street begging for change? How do they feel after interacting with me? How does my energy serve the world? How does my energy serve myself?

My life is 100% my responsibility. No more victim consciousness. No more imposed limitations from others. No more blaming someone else. No more believing someone is coming to save me. No more thinking someone messed up my life and put me into this position. I am a piece of consciousness part of the bigger collective consciousness of this planet. I am connected to every other piece of consciousness living inside every human and inside every animal. Inside each of our skin bags is the same consciousness that breathes us.

When I die I will return to this collective consciousness along with every other dead human and animal on the planet. So I know that every thing I think and do towards another is also affecting me and the collective consciousness of the planet. Everything and everyone are completely linked to each other. We are one! We are one alive consciousness that is breathing and living everything. Yes I really grasp this! I read these lines a few times over and over, so I really grasp this and LIVE this in my EVERY moment of the day! I take on a way bigger responsibility of putting out kindness, love and inspiration into my world so I can do my part in making this planet a more peaceful and happy place. I have the power to change the world by the energy I put out. Yes I am that powerful!

In every moment I can choose. I can choose to be kind or I can choose to be mean. I can choose to appreciate someone or I can dismiss them. I can bring joy or I can bring sorrow. I can hang on to old versions of others or I can see their transformations. I can hold my love prisoner or I can let it flow freely like a waterfall. I can continue believing the old limiting small and unworthy story of my life or I can create a new movie. I am the movie projector. Out of me comes my external reality. So what movie do I want to project? Is it a love story? A comedy? An adventure? A magical fantasy? What movie do I want to project for the next 3 years? For my lifetime? Can I visualize it down to the finest detail? Can I feel what it feels like? Taste it? Smell it? Can I get really clear on the reality I want?

WAIT, WHAT EXACTLY DO I WANT? ...

What Do I Want?

WHAT DO I WANT? HMMM.... KIND OF stumps me
doesn't it? What about, what kind of life do I want to
create? Can I see it in detail when I close my eyes to
visualize it? Can I order my life off a limitless universal menu
and know exactly what items I want on that menu? Am I clear
on how to visualize and dream up my future? Do I know what
kind of future I want? Can I see all the little details? Can I
touch it? Smell it? Taste it? What does it sound like? What are
the colors? What am I wearing? Where am I standing? Who
is with me? How do I feel?

What is the biggest dream I can dream up?

I don't know. I'm not sure. There are so many possibilities.
How do I choose? What do I want? Well it should be so simple
but I haven't given it much thought before. Hmmmm. It's so
hard to choose and narrow it down. I certainly know what I
DON'T want. I can make a long massive list there. I can go on
and on about what I don't want, but ask me what I want and I

feel stumped. I don't know why it scares me to dream this big. To dream it all up. Maybe I don't believe it's possible. Maybe I don't believe dreaming it will make any difference. Maybe I believe that I am just here to react to the life I was born into and the destiny that is already laid out for me and so I can just blindly continue to follow along, not have to think or really make much of an effort.

In a strange way, I would rather not know I am 100% in charge, so i can just keep sleeping and reacting to everything that comes my way. To hop into the driver's seat takes responsibility. It takes me getting clear and awake. It takes me making choices and choosing my fate. I am scared. What if I choose wrong? What if I mess up my life? What if I choose the wrong person to be with? So I will not choose. I will not choose anything because I am scared of being accountable to making a mistake. I will stay in the crappy relationship, crappy job or crappy apartment, because I fear choosing something else incase I choose it wrong and mess my life up. So I stay stuck. I say "I cannot choose, it is too scary". But the crazy thing is, I AM CHOOSING. By not choosing something different, I keep choosing my same situation. I always choose, even when I think it is being chosen for me. I am still ultimately in charge and I always have choice.

I can continue thinking life is just happening to me and I have no control of anything. It is not a free life, but it is a safe life. As long as I am ok with limitation and I am ok to keep my life small, then I will not question or awaken to the possibility that my life is 100% my responsibility and how it is turning out is completely in my control. However, if I do choose to believe that I am dreaming it up then my life becomes so much freer. I will no longer feel troubled with making choices and fearing choosing wrong. There is no wrong. There is no right. It is all just me dreaming it up into existence. Which partner I choose, what program I create for my business, where to take vacation, which dress to buy – no longer matter. I am dreaming it up, there is no right and there is no wrong. There is only what I choose to put my energy towards. There is only what I choose.

So as the dreamer weaving this movie into reality, I now make choices with confidence and get behind my choices. No one can tell me my choice is wrong, if in my heart I feel it is the right choice. I am in control of my choices and if they come from a deep intuitive knowing, then I confidently stand behind my heart's truth. If I feel excited about teaching children in a third world country, then no one can tell me whether this is a good business or career choice. Only I choose where to follow my passions and where I will be the greatest expression of myself. I choose something and go after it with all my passion. I see myself as already having it. It may take a little while for my external movie to catch up to my new way of thinking and being. It may take a little while for my attracting magnet to pull in my new desires and deliver them to me from the infinite cosmic universal menu. Eventually with enough of my mental mind power directed towards these dreams, I will be experiencing them soon enough.

This same level of mental mind power has been creating my reality until now and I have been unconscious to it. Up untill now I have been creating my life without knowing it. I have been thinking I was reacting to it instead. I have put mental energy

71

towards a belief, then eventually this belief played out and I said, "see I knew it would happen eventually. I always have bad luck." It's like I predicted what the universe was going to give me and I could prove I was right all along. The same breakup or the same cheating story, the same betrayal of a friend, the same old story, it just keeps playing out the same and I think I have bad luck. I think the universe doesn't like me or has it out for me. I think I am doomed. I think I have no hope yet I didn't realize that I have been unconsciously and subconsciously focusing my energy toward things that will bring me sorrow. When I keep focusing my energy and talking about what I don't want, I will get more of what I don't want. The universe says, "ok I will give you more of what you focus on!"

Am I still holding on to lingering old beliefs or victim consciousness that this happened to me and will happen to me again? Am I telling old stories over and over again to anyone who will listen? Why do I keep putting negative, unhappy, fearful energy towards creating the same crap in my life? Why am I still asleep to my magnificent manifesting power? Enough!!! I'm now waking up in my dream! I now recognize I am dreaming my life into reality in every second. I take ownership of my life. I ask myself what do I want and I get really clear on that. Then I jump into the driver's seat, strap on my seatbelt and put my life adventure into overdrive!

What do I want? In a relationship? In my career? In my life? Family? Friendships? Who do I want to be? What do I want to have? What do I want to dream into reality? Let the fun begin....

EXERCISE: WHAT DO I WANT?

1. I go sit alone in privacy. In my car works great. I drive somewhere or got sit in my car garage. I tilt the rearview mirror and look into it.

2. I get my smart phone voice memo recorder and hit record.

3. Now I speak out loud my life as if it is already in the future of what I want. I already have this. I am already this. I am making this much money already. I am married to so and so. I live in XYZ. As I want it and I can visualize it and then it is already so. I talk like I am speaking to someone or being interviewed about my life.

4. For example I say, " I have the most amazing extraordinary vibrant and energized life. I have so much energy. I bounce out of bed. I get on my yoga mat. I go for a walk in nature or I exercise in the back yard. I connect to myself every morning and appreciate myself. I check in with myself and make sure to give myself what it is I want and need for the day. I wake up with prayer and love in my heart to serve the world and I am inspired by my life. My business is thriving and I support people with my work. My way of being and my way of living inspires, supports, empowers and makes many people happy. I make a positive impact on the people I meet and on the sustainability of this planet. I have joy and peace in my heart. I have the most amazing team of people around me supporting my life and my business. Together we access bigger and bigger opportunities and doorways. I love being creative and collaborating with amazingly smart innovative people. I love creating incredibly

inspiring and transformational projects for the good of this planet and humankind. My life feels fulfilled every day, my life is action packed and my mind is filled with inspiration and imagination. I have the most amazing kind sexy compassionate amazing mature love partner on the planet. I am blessed that we have found each other and we are moving mountains together. We love and adore each other completely. We lift each other up in all ways. We are free, kind, collaborative, creative, grounded and connected. We travel to the most amazing places in the world for our vacations. I have an abundance of money and resources keep coming my way. I use some of this abundance to do more good on the planet and help other people. I am living my highest purpose. I am expressing myself in the fullest self expression of myself and I am the greatest version of myself in every moment. I love and adore myself. I grow in wisdom, connection, divinity, self love and compassion every day. I glow brighter and brighter. I beam my light bright, never again dimming. I am a light for all those around me. I love my life. I love my body. I love me."

5. I listen back to my recording. It will help me believe. It will help me connect to my wants and my life creation faster by hearing my own voice tell my own life story.

6. I record it again. This time with more clarity, more assurance and more knowing. I say it with more and more detail. I feel like it is already so. I have more faith in this exercise and in my life story. I believe more and more that it is my reality.

7. I keep playing this game and asking these questions in my head, "What do I want? How do I want it? Where do I want it? Who do I want it with?"

8. I STOP focusing on what I DON'T want. I catch myself every time I start telling someone or thinking, "I don't want this..." and quickly change it to "I want this...". This is the BIGGEST self catch I can do for myself. I catch myself and change my "I don't want" to "I want".

9. I close my eyes and meditate. I take a few moments to imagine what I want. I dream up my life in my imagination. I close my eyes and play a mini movie in my mind of how I want my life to be. How do I want to wake up in the morning? How do I want to feel? How do I want my day to unfold? I imagine my perfect day. I use all 5 senses inside my vision to lock in my dream.

10. I use a journal. I spend time making lists of what I want and how I want my life to be. What dreams and visions do I have? I draw it. Doodle it. Write about it. The more time, energy and detail I put into my dreams, the faster they start playing out on the big movie screen of my life. I make a list of my ideal partner and all their traits. How will I feel in their presence? What will we do together? I get detailed. If I am already in a relationship, then I find these traits in my partner? Can I support them to be their greatest version of themselves? Can I help my partner fulfill all their dreams, hopes and wishes? Can I lift my partner up, to their greatest empowerment and self expression?

I GET CLEAR ON WHAT I WANT
I PLAY WITH MY IMAGINATION
I FANTASIZE
I DREAM BIG
I VISION
I DREAM MY BIGGEST DREAM
I REMEMBER IT'S MY LIFE
I PLAY FULL OUT
I GET CLEAR NOW
WHAT HAVE I GOT TO LOSE?
EXCEPT YEARS OF MY LIFE

...

CHAPTER 14

I See The Signs

NOW THAT I AM FULLY ON BOARD and in agreement that I am creating my life, then this book has a delicious secret for me....The universe is helping me create my life too and is totally on my side. I am not alone! The universe wants me to be the best version of myself and to fulfill my soul's destiny. It is totally cheering me on and waiting for me to start shining brighter and brighter. The universe is waiting for me to get into the driver's seat, say yes to my life so it can continue showing me road signs and landmarks to make my journey easier, more guided and more connected. Now the difference is, I am FINALLY ready to see them.

My life is a miracle unfolding with magic and creation everywhere, I just have to look. I start looking for the landmarks and the signs from the universe. In the past, I have had coincidences happen to me. So I know there are "weird" things out there. I think of someone and they phone me. What a coincidence! I think of someone and run into them 'by chance' when I am out? Wow what a coincidence! I talk about an event with a friend and the event invite is at the top of my Facebook feed when I log on. Weird hey?! What a coincidence! I can't believe it! I tell my friends, again stating, "I can't believe it".

If I can't believe it, then I determine it to be so. I say it's not believable and so it is, as I declare it. My words are my spells and I determine my reality based on the words I use. I was not taught that there was magic at play in my life and that there is magic in the universe all around me. I was told my life was basic, that I have no power, that I am nothing really, that I am small, that I am NOT free and that I need a government, medical system, pharmaceuticals and poisonous food, poisonous water, poisonous air to survive.

I was told that only the church and the priest can connect to the divine magical universal energy and that I am a powerless sinful human, one that needs a priest to repent me and deem me worthy of my existence here on earth and then also in my heavenly or hellish afterlife. I was told I can't talk to the Divine Universal Energy directly because I lack the power and connection that only the priest has.

I was told that I don't have any higher powers of my own and that I am a mortal human, with no special power. I was also told I am powerless and my life is ordinary and will continue to be ordinary, till I die. I may attempt to do something extraordinary to shake my life up, but will most likely get no support from my fear filled families and communities who cannot imagine that all my "taught" limitations could actually be false and that I could in fact...

BE MORE POWERFUL THAN I WAS TAUGHT TO BELIEVE! Yes – this - is - very - possible - indeed!!!

I have been programmed to believe that my world is happening to me, that I just react to the world around me and that I have no power and then WOW this coincidence happens. For a second I think, "did I create that to happen just by thinking about it?" But quickly I shun that silly idea out of my mind and declare that I am just being silly, I can't make anything happen. I have no special super powers. I'm just a little wee human.

I am now stepping up my awareness, awakeness and trusting that the universe is giving me little signals and nudges to move me along. I am inviting myself to now see 'random' coincidences as synchronicities or 'meaningful' coincidences instead. I am no longer brushing them off as nothing. I now see them as signs the universe is giving me, to assure me she is playing right along side of me every step of the way.

I now watch for signs. I stop and observe them. I am in a state of wonder and awe of my life unfolding. I am inviting myself to slow down and look at the intricate spider web of life consciousness that I am a part of. I can think of someone across the world and they can feel my energy pop into their mind and they call me. I can send prayers to another part of the world and my energy will travel through the cosmic consciousness and reach its destination.

I will now question my dreams more and question the signs all around me. I am in wonder. I ponder. I reflect. I take time to see the signs. The more I take time to witness the signals and the messages, the more magical my life starts to feel. The more I feel guided and connected to something bigger than myself, the more I can release and trust in my life unfolding. I like feeling connected to a bigger universe looking out for me. She is taking care of me and moving me along to become the biggest full bloom of myself possible. She is helping me radiate my biggest light from inside out, encouraging me to do what ever LIGHTS me up!!!

So now, more than ever, I believe in magic and the universe dropping me love notes. What about miracles? What do I think of miracles? Bible Church stuff and not even in my reality? Think they are woo woo? Or a daily miracle user and use them all the time?

At first it may be hard to believe that miracles or sparkles of magic are even possible, yet believing makes my life way more fun. Miracles and magic are happening in my life daily, moment by moment and I can tap into them when ever I want. I can ask for a miracle. Every day. All the time. For every situation. For every concern. For every loss. For every sorrow. For every heart ache. For every longing. Every needing. Every desiring. Every dreaming. Every creating. Every time I need the help of someone or something outside of me.

Every time I need a little support, encouragement and divine intervention I can ask for a miracle. The divine is here for me. The universe has my back and is supporting me in every moment.

How do I ask for a miracle?

It's simple I ask and know it is my divine birthright to be able to do so. It is my birthright as a miraculous energetic conscious magical spark of life Being on this planet to remember that I am part of the collective life force Divine Energy that permeates everything including my body.

I am part of the one spark of life that births and breathes everything. It is my birthright to ask for a miracle to help me in my human existence on this planet. My soul asks for miracles. I am not selfish. I am not greedy. I am not taking more than my share. I ask for miracles because it is part of my existence on this planet to use miracles as tools for my healing and my thriving. There is an infinite supply of miracles floating around and I now start asking and receiving my boundless share.

As I ask for miracles and I see the signs, my life becomes much more connected and magical every step of the way. I practice and keep opening up to new ways of up leveling my life to a super human level.

EXERCISE: SEEING THE SIGNS

1. I get a journal. I write in it. I am aware of my life journey daily.

2. I wake up to my life mystery unfolding. I don't fall back asleep.

3. I watch who comes across my path. I watch my interactions. I watch my manifestations. I watch the dance of my life dancing in front of me, with more awareness and connection than ever before.

4. Numbers can be seen as little kisses from the universe. Seeing 11:11 everywhere. Or 444, 555 or 333 and any other patterns of numbers that pop up in the perfect opportune moments, can feel like a gentle kiss from the universe telling me I am on track.

5. I catch every time I excuse something as a random act, coincidence or weird thing that happened. I catch patterns that continue showing up and I am in wonder about them instead of dismissing them like I used to in the past.

6. I walk my life path as a warrior. I am aware of every twig snapping and every bush rustling. I spot tracks in the dirt and I watch for the clues like a detective. I am seeing the pieces coming together as the universe presents the signs to me.

7. I develop my muscle of trust. The more I trust the universe, the more I will see the signs she is giving me.

8. I live in the present moment. In the Now Now Now! I will miss the signs if I am living in the past or the future. When my mind is focused elsewhere in some illusionary world of the past or future, I am not focusing on the world in front of me. I cannot see what the universe is presenting to me or hear my soul speaking if I am not in the present moment.

9. Is the world a bad place or a good place? My answer to this most important question determines the kind of signs I see in my life and the kind of experience of life I have. A massive journey into my self love and self peace is to shift this perception of how I view the world. If I look for flowers and beauty, I will find flowers and beauty. If I look for hate and fear, I will find hate and fear. I choose how I want to see the world by changing how I focus my lens and belief system.

10. How I see others is the same thing. I can focus on someone's dark and negative attributes and see that. Or I can focus on all their good and their light and see that. I can create a totally different person, based on where I focus my view of them.

11. I connect myself to magic and to the signs and whispers of the universe. Why not? It's way more fun. It's the wonder I had as a child, where I played and lived in complete unity with the universe and everything all around me. Back then I was free and trusted the magic of every day unfolding. I take on this level of wonder once again.

I SEE THE SIGNS

AS KISSES FROM THE UNIVERSE

I FEEL CONNECTED

TO A BIGGER MAGIC

THE BIGGER MAGIC OF THE UNIVERSE

ALL THE PLANETS

ALL THE STARS

ALL THE GALAXIES

ALL THE CREATURES

ALL THE PLANTS

ALL THE ROCKS A

ALL THE WATER SOURCES

I FEEL PART OF EVERYTHING

THE UNIVERSE HAS MY BACK

MY LIFE IS FUN

I TRUST

...

CHAPTER 15

Trust. I Release. I Receive.

OW MUCH DO I TRUST THE UNIVERSE and my existence on this planet to be taken care of? How much do I believe I am safe?

I have not been taught to feel safe in my own body, in my own life and in my own reality. I have not been taught by the school system that the universe has my back and is waiting for me to start co-creating with it. I was not told of my own power and my ability to create my own reality.

Feeling safe and taken care of is very important for my internal peace of mind and happiness in my life. People sometimes get into relationships just for the feeling of safety and protection. People don't go on vacations or venture out to explore the world because they fear for their safety on this planet. I have been brainwashed to fear the world out there and to fear my existence in it. I might see the world as a bad unsafe place and not believe I am being taken care of and provided for. The less I trust, the less I feel safe in this world. The less I feel safe in this world, the less I will follow my dreams and ambitions since I won't trust the universe to help me make them happen. Learning trust is VERY important.

Trust is not something I can gain just by reading about it. I have to begin to feel it first or start to see it in my daily life. I look back at moments in my life and see examples where I realize I was taken care of. Just when I thought I would be stranded at the party, I meet someone who lives right by me and gives me a lift home. Just when I thought I wouldn't have money to pay my rent, I land a new client. Just when I thought my breakup with X was the end of the world, I meet Y around the corner and find the love of my life.

My favorite new saying is;
"Could be bad, could be good, too early too tell".

I trust all is unfolding for my highest good.
I trust the universe has my back.
I trust myself to create an amazing life for myself.
I trust.
I order my dreams, visions, goals, plans, manifestations & creations off the magical Universe menu.
Then I release. I wait. Then I receive.
It's like when I go for dinner. I go to my favorite restaurant and I order food from the menu.
I get clear on what I want. I order.

I then trust this order will be given to the kitchen.
I release and continue having a fun chatting with my friends.
I trust my food is on its way to me.
I receive my meal.

Once I get clear and order, I release and let the restaurant take care of my wishes. I trust the kitchen and surrender. I know the restaurant has my back and will serve me the best food possible. This is the same with my life. The more I trust, the more freedom I have to dream knowing the universe is there to assist me in fulfilling my orders. The more I can trust the universe, the more she will help me in my full blossoming.

Every flower in nature, every fruit, every seed has within it a program to bring itself to its greatest expression on the planet and it's full blossoming. I too have this same program within me. I am already destined for my greatest full self expression, my path is already laid out and I am playing out my destiny.

The question is, can I get my life back on its highest destiny track and become the greatest expression of myself? Will I give myself permission to take 100% responsibility and live out my special purpose on this planet? Will I say yes to my greatest potential or will I say yes to my lowest potential? I choose.

My life is destined for greatness and fullest expression and it is up to me to meet the universe there. It is up to me if I do something meaningful with my life or not. It is up to me if I listen to my heart and soul's longing. It is up to me if I act on it. It's in there. Speaking to me. Whispering. Screaming. Trying to get my attention. It is up to me if I listen. The universe is holding me in my biggest light and sees me as great, even before I do. It knows my full potential to be happy and thriving on this planet. It is up to me to say yes. It is up to me to paddle towards the wave every day if I want to ride it. The wave is there ready for me, I just have to make a little effort to meet it.

I TRUST
I RELEASE
I RECEIVE

KNOWING THE UNIVERSE HAS MY BACK!

CHAPTER 16

I Forgive

ONE OF THE GREATEST TOOLS I CAN MASTER on this planet is the art of forgiveness.

Perhaps I am hanging on to old wounds, hurts, resentments, fights, arguments, disagreements, issues, miscommunications and guilt. So much pain and body dis-ease comes from these low vibration frequencies filling my body with turmoil and angst.

A brilliant saying is "holding on to anger and resentment towards someone is like drinking poison and expecting the other to die".

This says that if I hold on to resentment and contempt for someone, I am the one actually being poisoned by this action, not them. I am the one hanging on. I am constantly thinking about this. I am the one stressing over it or it's playing in the background of my mind and I am subconsciously poisoning my day with it. My body is stressed by this. My mind is not at peace. My heart is closed off.

I get to choose if I close off the valve of love flowing from my heart or keep it open. I can flow love even to those who have scorned me or hurt me. My life is about my own personal healing journey and if resentment causes harm in my body then I choose to let it go and set my heart free. I can forgive someone. I might not agree with what they did or said. I might choose to never see them again and I can forgive them and release them from my energetic hold. I can stop sending negative energy their way and I can release this negative energy out of my body. I am committed to showing up as a bigger form of love for myself and for others. I forgive and no longer hold on to old low vibration pain inside my body. I stop keeping my body prisoner to my resentful and angry mind. I release the pain, old stories and I learn to forgive. I learn to move on, to let go and I am free!!!

A lack of forgiveness is what creates sickness in my body. I know there are many other factors that contribute to sickness, yet forgiveness is the most powerful and effective way to my self healing and life thriving on this planet. If I am hanging on to stuff towards another and I haven't moved past this, seen this person in love and compassion, healed the charge inside my own body and become a bigger love in the world because of this, then I have work to do. Forgiving can be really hard. Forgiving a rapist, murderer, liar, cheater, back stabber is really hard! I am not saying what they did was right or ok. Yet truly, I am not healing this for them, I am healing this for me. I am healing this pain that is living inside me. This energetic hurtful angry pain that is potentially causing me harm and affecting my life in all areas.

So it's time to forgive as a gift to me. I start out by making this forgiveness about setting ME FREE first and then ideally setting the OTHER FREE too. If I want to go to the super human level of LOVE on this planet, then I release the energy I am holding over us and I set us free. I set us free to live out our karma and our life dream on this planet. Perhaps my forgiveness sends the other a vibration of such positivity, that they change their life around, start saving the world and making a massive difference in healing humanity. Perhaps my forgiveness was the energy that set that magical spark forth and helped them heal their own life. Yes I am that powerful!

Forgiving myself for all my mistakes and wrong doings is equally important. Actually even more crucial than forgiving others is starting with forgiving myself first. I deserve to be forgiven. I deserve to be let off the hook. I deserve for the self-inflicted mental punishment to end. I deserve internal piece in my world and I deserve to be forgiven, for whatever wrong doing I did; For who ever I hurt; For what ever I took that was not mine; For all the damage I have caused; All the hearts I have broken; All the pain I have caused; All the time I have wasted; All the ways I have made myself small; All the ways I've hidden in bed rather than going out to impact society; For all my fears; For all my insecurities; For all my silly beliefs that I am not a good enough person; For feeling unworthy to ask for the raise; For feeling unworthy enough to ask my crush out; And for feeling too insignificant to ask for what I deserve.

I give forgiveness to myself for not speaking my truth. I give forgiveness to myself for all the times I've kept quiet when inside I was screaming. Forgiveness for worrying about someone else's feelings, more than my own. Forgiveness for all the times I didn't stand by my beliefs for fear of not being liked or accepted. Forgiveness for the times I gave my heart to someone not quite so worthy. Forgiveness for all the stress I've caused myself and others. Forgiveness for not loving and adoring myself all these years, for beating myself up, for saying nasty things to myself, for fighting for my limitations and forgiveness to my self for feeling not good enough.

I now say, I am sorry! I am truly sorry! I am sooooo sorry! I now make myself #1! I live my life like my every thought, action and word I speak means something, because it does. I am my most important person because this is my reality, my dream, my movie. I live my life with this awareness and practice creating my reality moment by moment. I wake up in my own life dream, I forgive and I let go of all my crap so I can live a more juicy vibrant extraordinary life.

So how do I forgive? It is not easy. If I am brewing with anger, contempt, jealousy, fear, insecurity, hurt, pain and despair, it is very difficult to calm down and release to another state of happier being. So it might take time. Maybe I need a few days to brew in my anger. Maybe a few hours or a few moments. The name of the game is how quickly can I get off my racket of someone and move to forgiveness and love.

If I am spending time with the person that has angered me, I usually need an acknowledgement or apology from that person to feel complete. I do my best to calm my energy so I am not lashing out asking for the apology.

I say: "Hey I don't like the way you just spoke to me and my feelings are hurt. I don't think you would try and hurt me, but I am feeling really hurt. Can you help me heal this pain I feel in my heart right now. I would like you to hear me and to apologize."

Being able to speak like the above is ideal, usually I am too upset and say something like: "You jerk. That was so rude what you just said to me. I'm super hurt. You hurt me. Why are you so rude to me? What is your problem?"

Both conversations mean the same thing, but one might create an apology and the other most likely a war. If who I'm speaking to is easily triggered, on the edge, egoic, unapproachable or just a jerk, then no matter how I bring something up, they will get triggered and let out a roar. Some people will not like me speaking my truth or confronting their attitude or behavior. Most people don't want to be called out on their behavior or have to look at their own crap. Most likely, they have been hiding from it for so long and pretending their crap does not exist. So if I raise awareness to their behavior, they get angry and feel forced to look at their shadows. I might not get the apology I am looking for.

Approaching and trying to heal with people might cause me a lot of pain and crying. Some people are mean, they are like fearful animals that have been abused and beaten by life. They are shaking at the back of their cages. Even if I put my hand in there with love and food, they might bite my hand off. There is only so much I can do for some people and not everyone wants to wake up. Not everyone wants to be 100% accountable. Not everyone wants to be elevated. Not everyone wants to be healed. Not everyone wants to evolve or thrive on this planet. Some people feel happier clinging on to the shore fearing the current of the stream. Some of us feel the calling to let go of the shore, float in the current and trust the current will take us where we need to go and some will continue clinging.

It is I who can forgive, write a new story, release the energy I hold over someone and open up the valve of my heart, so my heart energy flows once more. Holding my heart valve shut and not allowing love energy to flow, can cause sickness inside my body. Heart sickness, a broken heart or heart disease are blocked energy flows. So how am I moving the energy of my heart?

I am made up of energy. Energy flows throughout my skin body bag and activates all my body functions. I am so talented and can multi task many things at the same time. I can read, chew gum, sing and skip all at once. Simultaneously my hair and nails are growing, my organs are pumping and cleansing my body, my blood is running, my eyes are blinking, my mouth is swallowing saliva and mucous is forming in my head and flowing down my nose without me having to do anything. Wow my body is so miraculous!

Energy is flowing through me, all around me and in everything I encounter. I am an energetic being living in an energetic world. I am a piece of the whole consciousness that creates and moves everything. I am one small piece of a whole big thing. I am connected.

Now imagine what happens when I close off my heart valve energy towards a person or a situation or an organization. All this energy inside of me that wants to flow is being stopped. Stopped valves inside my heart that are not being allowed to flow will eventually erupt. So the faster I can open up my heart, forgive and let go, the faster I will transform my life and create bigger inner healing.

Here are some amazing exercises to learn forgiveness. They are helpful and effective in helping me let go of the crap I am carrying around inside my heart, my mind, my soul and my body. These exercises do not require the person I am forgiving to be present. I can do all these exercises sitting alone.

In these forgiveness techniques it's about being willing. Willing to let go of the toxic sludgy resentment that is poisoning my body. Willing to let go of the energetic pain that has been holding my body and heart prisoner. I release. I find compassion. I find love. I see myself as a bigger source of love than the person that wronged me. I find it in my heart to forgive and not take it personally.

EXERCISE 1: FORGIVENESS – BYRON KATIE "THE WORK"

Byron Katie has written several books and can be found on YouTube. Most effective way to absorb and use this forgiveness tool is for me to get her books on audio and listen to them while walking in nature. In my car also works well, but forgiveness energy is diluted with my driving alertness.

1. I get her books on audio.

2. I go on www.byronkatie.com and download the 4 question worksheets. The 4 questions are: *Is it true? - *Can I absolutely know that it's true? – *How do you react, what happens, when I believe that thought? – *Who would I be without the thought?

3. I check out her website and YouTube videos for extra help. I listen to the audio books and do the worksheets for this process to really be effective.

4. I am ready for a healing. I am willing to look at myself. I am willing to let go of ego and step into compassion. I am willing to shift my perspective and alleviate pain and suffering for myself and others.

EXERCISE 2: FORGIVENESS - HO'OPONOPONO

Ancient Hawaiian conflict resolution and forgiveness tool still used in ceremonies today but unfortunately not practiced by every day Hawaiians. Works with energy and moving it to a higher vibration.

1. Words are "I'm sorry. I love you. Please forgive me. Thank you". In any order that feels right. No right or wrong.

2. I don't have to see the person I am forgiving or even be around them. This is MY own practice I create with myself to move my own energy. It will also help move the energy I hold over someone and create a shift inside them.

3. I close my eyes. I visualize this person.

4. I chant the mantra over and over and over and over and over again. "I'm sorry. I love you. Please forgive me. Thank you"

5. I focus on shifting my own vibration as my body moves from a state of contraction to expansion.

6. I focus on shifting the energy I have towards this person as I let go of the negative energetic charge I was sending their way.

7. When I release it all in the energetic field and I forgive it in the ethereal realm, then I will see it transform in the physical world. It's amazing and magical at the same time how much this practice works.

EXERCISE 3: FORGIVENESS - VISUALIZATION

Using my imagination and my mind to create this next level of healing. Allowing myself to connect within and remember that I have the power to transform and alchemize anything within me, this is my dream and my reality.

1. I close my eyes. I breathe. I IMAGINE the person in front of me. Sitting silently in a chair. I sit in a chair opposite them. Quite close.

2. I use my imagination and make this real. This is energetically really happening. This person is sitting right in front of me.

3. I focus on their face. I stare at their face. I say nothing. I don't feel forced to speak. If something comes up great but I am not doing the talking. I sit patiently. I feel into my body and my feelings.

4. I keep looking at the person in my imagination. I ask them, "do you have anything to say?" "Do you need to apologize to me for anything?" "What is really going on for you?" "What do you want to tell me?"

5. Now I listen. I don't force it. I just patiently listen.

6. At first I might not hear anything. It is in fact my inner voice that will do the talking so I don't rush it and I let it speak. I don't second guess the answers or hush the voice. I just listen. I let my soul speak. It usually knows the answers and energetically my soul can answer for the other person.

7. I might feel called to speak too. To tell the person something. To apologize or to speak my truth. I let what ever needs to come, come.

8. Ideally I close out my time with this person and feel lighter and freer. Ideally some form of energy shift has happened.

I FORGIVE
I LET GO
I GIVE LOVE

...

CHAPTER 17

I Let Go Of My Crap

L ETTING GO OF MY OWN CRAP CAN BE the hardest thing for me to face and do in this lifetime. Let's face it, I cling to my crap both inside and outside my body. I clutter my home and my life with crap. I clutter my body and colon with crap. I feel burdened and weighed down by my crap. I actually do hate having to carry it all around. Moving it from place to place. Dusting it. Storing it. Worrying about it.

My body is definitely full of crap. If I eat cooked food, meat, dairy, processed food, chemicals and preservatives, then I definitely have crap inside my body. My fecal matter is made up of 50% food and 50% dead cells. Since my cells are dying in every second, I am constantly making new poo. My crap is weighing me down and making me slower in all ways. It makes my mind foggier and my body into a toxic wasteland swamp.

I hate to think about or talk about pooping. Shouldn't it just all work down there? Well yes it should but most of us are constipated. Clinging. Clenching. Holding on to. Fearing letting go. All this crap is making all of us sick. Constipation is the No. 1 disease facing most of the world. Everyone has too much crap inside of them and it's making them fat, bloated and sick. Crap is polluting our blood, our body fluids, our organs and our mind. Most of us have an internal toxic swamp and this accounts for most dis-ease of the body and mind.

My external crap makes me sick too. I visually see it and physically feel the energy of the extra crap all around me. I might not be aware of it, but all this stuff gives me subtle anxiety, feels unsettling and creates upheaval inside me. When I open the closet doors, I quickly close them as I see all my crap overflowing. When I go in to the garage, I get overwhelmed with all the crap stored in there and have to walk away. When I get into my messy full of crap car, I do not feel at peace and usually apologize with embarrassment to anyone I give a ride to.

I might even have a storage locker where I am storing more crap and it gives me stress thinking I will have to sort through it one day. Every corner of my house might be packed with crap. I might see it as keep sakes, souvenirs and things I will use one day so I can't get rid of anything. Yet all my stuff is taking up energetic space in my life and new energy cannot flow in. Not to mention all the dust it's collecting that I can't clean fast enough, which creates more stress.

My internal crap makes me sick and my external crap makes me unsettled, yet I continue to cling to it, as if without it I would be nothing. Who would I be without all my stuff? Who would I be without all my excess weight? Who would I be if I was lighter? What if I was freer? What if I started floating on life, living in a new realm of bliss and enlightenment by letting go of all the heavy stuff? What would happen then? Like in a hot air balloon, if I want the balloon to lift up fast, I have to throw overboard all the heavy stuff and my balloon will very quickly levitate. It's the same with my body, my mind and my life. To levitate higher I have to toss the crap overboard. I now have the tools here in this book, on how to levitate myself up. I now do the work to get myself lighter.

What if I purged my crap and became a more amazing shiny vibrant charged up version of me? Who could I be? Who do I dare to be? A shinier, more vibrant healthier version of me? Am I brave enough to take responsibility for my life and finally choose me first? Can I finally choose my dreams, my visions, my adventures, my journeys, my freedom, my sovereignty, my inner peace and my most extraordinary juicy vibrant life ever? Am I ready for this?

Letting go of my crap is vital to living a freer more extraordinary juicy vibrant peaceful healthy life. But wait, I'm good at crap removal. I spring clean. I go through my closet. I recycle. I keep my house clutter free. I drink a fiber scraping cleansing green smoothie every morning. I think I've got my crap under control. Or do I?

Well, this book is inviting me to amp up my crap body removal actions to the next level. To add in a higher level of cleansing that will actually move me into the "very healthy" category instead of the "pretty healthy" category. This book is inviting me to move from level 1 to level 5 of extraordinary, if I want to create anything major inside my life and inside my body.

Time to stop playing small. If I want to be the greatest expression of myself on this planet and perhaps help people in some way, then I have to get myself to that super human level so I can spread more of my good in the world. I am committed to feeling good in my life and to people feeling good in my presence. I am committed to my body feeling amazing so I love it, forgive it, adore it and feed it the most nourishing juicy food possible.

I am being asked to amp up my internal and external cleansing routines to the next level and to move the energy inside my body and inside my home. To clean, dust, de-clutter, open windows and move furniture. To move energy inside my mind that is storing too much crap and let go of the anger and resentment. I scream. I beat pillows. I see a shrink. I do forgiveness exercises. I cleanse my heart from holding on to old wounds and I open up the valve for love to flow. I give myself love and kindness to truly cleanse myself of the self loathing thoughts and from now on only allow the self loving ones in.

My world is full of toxins. Poisonous gases and fumes in my air. Poisonous chemicals and toxins in my water. Poisonous pesticides in my food. My body is poisoned by the environment, by the pharmaceutical drug companies, by big corporations, by pesticide and chemical manufacturers and by my lack of education on these subjects. My mind is poisoned by the brainwashing media and by the mindless numbing television reality programs. My soul is poisoned by the lack of respect, sovereignty and dumbing down oppression inflicted upon me by society and the system.

I can continue hanging on to my crap until it poisons my body and my life OR I can become more open to cleansing, letting go and releasing old stagnant energy so new energy has room to enter.

EXERCISE 1: LETTING GO OF CRAP IN MY HOUSE

1. I go into my bathroom and clean out all my cupboards. Pull everything out. Go through it. Give away what I don't use. My unwanted stuff is someone else's treasure. I throw away toxic creams and lotions, my skin is my biggest organ so anything I put on it, within 20 min will be swimming in my blood stream.

2. I go through my closet and try my clothes on. If they are not sexy or flattering or don't make me feel excited to put them on, then I get rid of them. I stop hanging on to something that I look hideous in, just because someone bought it for me or because it was expensive and I think I shouldn't throw it out. I wear flattering clothes. I wear comfortable clothes. I wear clothes I feel confident and good in. I wear clothes made from yummy soft eco friendly fabric that feel good on my skin. I get rid of the itchy synthetic my-crotch-can't-breathe yoga pants or underwear and buy cotton, bamboo or hemp instead.

3. I go through my jars and plastic containers. I search for

the lids. I match up my sets. I recycle the extras. I de-clutter the rest of my kitchen drawers and cupboards. I feel a sense of peace when I open my drawers and cupboards that have been cleaned and de-cluttered.

4. I read the ingredients of every package in my kitchen. If it has chemicals, preservatives, food colorings, high fructose corn syrup, canola oil, m.s.g., aspartame or other crap I can't pronounce or understand, I get rid of it. I cannot be truly loving myself if I put toxic food into my body. Food is my fuel. My blood, cells, organs and lymph fluid is made up of the fuel I put into my body. I love myself and feed myself the best fuel possible.

5. Am I surrounded by dust? When I have too much stuff, there's more space for dust and dirt to collect. I get rid of more stuff. I wipe the dust. I stop breathing in this dead dusty air and also stop sleeping in it. I sweep, wipe down surfaces and keep my house fresh and dust free (of course as much as possible – dust can build up way too fast to keep up).

6. I donate old books, magazines, dvds and cds to the library, old folks home or a charity thrift store. If I am no longer using it, watching it or interacting with it, then it's just collecting dust and it's better I get rid of it.

7. I go through my fridge, freezer and cupboards. If it's old, freezer burnt, has mites in it, has been sitting in my cupboards since before I can remember then I throw it out. Food has a shelf life. Spices are my medicine and if my medicine is old, it will no longer be as potent. Food sitting for months in plastic

bags takes on the properties of the plastic bag and can make my food rancid. I move my plastic bagged food into glass storage containers. I take care to preserve the freshest quality of my food so I can feed myself the best. I save glass jars from food, wash them and use them to store my spices, nuts, seeds, flours, sugars, etc. I am careful to not over hoard glass jars however, as this is a guilty pleasure of many people.

8. I open up the energy flow of my house. What do I mean by this? Well if every corner has stuff in it, if there is clutter everywhere then new energy cannot come in. New energy has no room to land, so it does not enter. My house and my life are most likely full of dead old stuck energy. I move furniture, remove storage boxes, de clutter the cupboards, move out old statues and picture frames and get rid of anything that no longer makes my heart skip into excitement when I see it. If I dislike the portrait hanging in my living room and it gives me a bad feeling when ever I see it, then I get rid of it. Even if I am not consciously aware of this, subconsciously I see everything around me and it either brings me joy and peace or stress.

9. I pick up each piece of art, decoration, equipment and novelty in my house, look at it, touch it and notice how it makes me feel. Is it bringing me joy or a sense of underlying unhappiness? If that old picture frame that my ex partner gave me, brings me annoyance and agitation every time I look at it, then I get rid of it. Who cares if it was expensive? Who cares if it was a gift? If it doesn't lift my vibration, then I get rid of it.

10. I change my cleaning products to non-toxic healthy eco-

green ones. I stop chemical air fresheners. I stop chemical sprays. I stop fake perfume laundry detergent. I clean up the quality of my air where I live and sleep. All these synthetic chemical smells can lead to irritation of my nasal passages, throat and lungs. When these synthetic chemicals touch my skin, they absorb and are swimming in my blood stream within 20 minutes. I might not notice the harshness of these chemicals if my body has gotten used to them, but as I switch to healthier options, I will notice the difference all natural makes.

11. I clean up my drinking water. I have healthy water inside my house. I have chlorine filters on all my showers. I make my drinking water my priority. I buy a counter filter jug or get a full filtration system or I go collect my own spring water. The spring water is molecularly structured for my body to understand and will hydrate and heal me the fastest. Water is liquid gold. Water is life. I make it a priority to have clean raw fresh drinking water as part of my lifestyle from now on. Ideally I find spring water, go collect it or have it delivered. I know this is the best most nutritious and energizing water for my body. Spring water is the fastest way to my healing, awakening and hydration. Once my body blood is made up of the earths' spring water, I vibrate at a different energy and am so much more connected to the planet. I can find springs at www.findaspring.com or I ask around.

Maybe I take my extra food, clothes, housewares, etc. to a shelter, food bank or to the single mom down the street. Perhaps my de-cluttering can really help someone else in need and make their day.

EXERCISE 2: LETTING GO OF CRAP IN MY FRIDGE AND MY BODY

This is one of the hardest places for me to start. I love my food and the comfort feelings it gives me. Making food changes is difficult for everyone, not just me. Unfortunately, some people would rather die then change their eating habits, even if these habits are what is killing them. Not me. I will not die or be unhealthy. I know it will be work for me to change to healthier eating habits and I also know that this change is the most essential for a healthy thriving life. My body is my machine and if it's toxic and broken then it can't function well for me. So I have to clean my body machine in order to heal disease and also live a thriving life. Food is my fuel. If I put crap into my body, then my body will be made of crap. As time goes by, my body will no longer be able clean itself if it is too overloaded with the crap I am ingesting. My body gets toxic, over burdened and poisoned. It starts to be in dis-ease.

This is where Petra's coaching and all her online programs can help me. She specializes in detox, healing the body, letting stuff go, reversing disease, prevention, mindfulness and of course self love. I can find all of Petra's online programs and free training at www.EatJuicy.com

I remember that this journey I am on is about self love and I love myself by taking care of myself starting now. Knowledge is power. I learn as much as I can and take my health into my hands.

1. I start with drinking green smoothies every morning. I join *Petra's Everything You Need To Know To Be Healthy & Thriving* to make this shift to a healthier lifestyle simple and doable for myself. Petra will guide me with simple easy steps and practices in eating, grocery shopping, mindfulness, exercise and self love. I am ready to change my life, have more energy, lose my excess weight, heal my gut and cleanse my body. I don't have to be confused with the latest diet fads, counting calories or feeling overwhelmed by the conflicting information on the internet. Petra has got my back by teaching me everything I need to know about being healthy, starting with setting up my day for success. I will be the best version of myself. I can start here: www.GreenSmoothieGangster.com

2. I stop eating anything processed or chemical filled. If I can't pronounce or understand the ingredients of a product, I don't eat it. I stop eating white sugar, white flour, white salt, soda pop, gluten, dairy, cheese, meat, eggs or I reduce them as much as possible. Most likely my body is allergic or does not react well to these foods. Ideally, I switch to a more raw food plant based vegan lifestyle! I start eating as many raw fruits and vegetables as possible. I learn how to master getting healthy in the kitchen and learn to cook delicious healthier meals. I stop all food colorings, canola oil, high fructose corn syrup, aspartame, artificial sweeteners, crappy vitamins, and anything else I intuitively know is crap. Food colorings affect my brain, nervous system and are very harmful to my body. I read ingredients of everything before I buy it and vote with my dollar wisely.

3. At least once per year or a few times per year, I give my body a break from digesting so it can focus all of its energy on healing me. When my body stops digesting food, it will spend all of its time on cleaning and healing. Drinking liquids in the form of juices, smoothies, soups, teas, water and super food elixirs will also hydrate my cells and help me reverse aging. Cleansing does not have to be scary or made into a big deal. I can add in more liquids and juicy food, my body will naturally cleanse and flush itself out. Again Petra can help me to do this safely, effectively and economically with her online juice cleansing programs and in person retreats.

4. If I have cancer or a major disease then I will want to cleanse my body and get rid of my physical and mental crap as fast as possible. Most likely my body is over burdened with toxins and the cells are not functioning properly. Cancer cells refuse to die because their off switch is broken, unlike healthy cells that die and regenerate constantly. When I hydrate my body with liquids and mass nutrition, my toxins begin to flush out and my cancer cells become responsive again. Cancer healing is not just about nutrition and cleansing, it is also very mental, physical and spiritual. Flushing my body however, will boost my immune system, help my body start functioning optimally again and give me a better chance at healing myself naturally. I don't have to feel alone and think I have to figure it all out. There is a lot of information out there and it can feel overwhelming. I spend my time healing my cancer, not trying to decipher information on the internet. If I want some support on learning how to heal myself naturally and not feel overwhelmed with all the information out there, then I will get Petra's help. She will share with me her 15 years of natural cancer healing information,

techniques, practices, recipes, resources and a healing plan for me to follow so I can learn how to use my body's own innate healing system to heal the cancer out of my body and have it never come back. Cancer healing is a full body, mind, heart and soul healing journey. I give myself permission to receive support, knowledge, confidence, faith and also be part of a community of people on the same healing journey.

5. Sometimes trying to do this level of crap removal at home by myself can feel challenging. Sometimes hopping on a plane to immerse myself into this type lifestyle is what my heart really wants. If I need support cleansing myself on all levels, doing it with someone and love being in paradise, then I can join Petra for a private or group retreat in the magical healing island of Bali Indonesia, where she lives. A journey to my self, a healing on a soul and heart level, an up leveling like no other, a cleansing and body healing that will reboot my entire system and create a deeper connection to my self in one of the most amazing magical healing places on the planet. Yes I am totally worthy!

6. Getting rid of my crap physically and emotionally is how I will heal and thrive in my lifetime. If I have not been taught how to do this, then it can feel challenging or daunting to understand this process. Instead of spending hours and hours trying to figure it out, I allow myself to receive the best guidance and support from Petra's online coaching programs and free training on her Facebook page and YouTube channel. Lots of healthy recipes, ongoing support, grocery shopping tips, inspiration, empowerment, self love guidance, self healing techniques and tons of tools to live a juicy vibrant extraordinary lifestyle.

7. Starting today, I begin eating more raw fruits and veggies in my new juicy lifestyle. I eat more whole real food. Rice pasta. Rice crackers. Rice bread. Corn tortillas. Kale, lots and lots of kale. Greens. Green smoothies. Plant based protein smoothies. Quinoa. Coconut milk. Almond milk. Nuts. Seeds. Lentils. Chickpeas. Beans. Seaweeds. Spices. Medicinal mushrooms. Fresh juices. Tahini. Almond butter. Raw cacao. Coconut oil. Teas. Hemp seeds. Chia seeds. Flax seeds. Kick ass salads with kicks ass healing salad dressings. Blender made raw soups and raw dips. I start taking better care of my body right now because I absolutely love and adore myself and I am totally worth it.

8. Not only do I drink coffee, but I put coffee up my butt to cleanse my bowel and my liver. I do coffee enemas and warm water enemas. I have colonics. I take magnesium supplements. I drink and eat raw chocolate and activated charcoal to move my bowel along. I use a pooping stool. I clean my colon. The colon is the king to my entire system, so its health will determine the health of the rest of my body. If it is full of excess fecal matter or resembles a toxic sewage swamp, then I take action to clean it. My toxic colon will create sickness in the rest of my body if left unattended. I flush my body with liquids and plant based fiber to get rid of my crap in my intestines and my bowel, as fast as possible.

9. I heal my gut. I heal my inflammation. I heal my acid reflux. I heal my heart burn. I heal my fire. My gut is the queen to my system. It must be full of good bacteria for me to have a healthy thriving body. Most likely my gut is toxic and overgrown with bad bacteria. This bad bacteria creates candida (yeast overgrowth) in my body, which some doctors say is at the

stem of sickness including cancer. This bad bacteria causes my skin issues, problematic hair, mood swings, mental imbalances, bad food cravings (especially sugar) and keeps my body a breeding ground for disease to set in. There are many ways to heal my gut naturally and I make healing this organ a priority. Petra's program can definitely help me if I need guidance.

11. I heal the relationship with myself and get rid of my self limiting, self diminishing and self hating crap. Issues live in my tissues. My self image, self beliefs and self imposed limitations can keep me toxic despite my cleansing efforts. My mind is very, very, very powerful. It is what controls all the functions of my body and my ultimate healing. If my mind declares, without a doubt, that I will be healthy, then I will be. If my mind declares that I am sick, that this cancer will kill me or I can't ever get better, then I will be. That is the power of my mind in my life and in my body healing. So eating salads isn't going to do much if I am speaking nasty toxic disempowering thoughts to myself. I heal my relationship with me and release all the toxic self-imposed crap I have been putting myself through and release it out of my mind.

12. My self-imposed crap could also be keeping me fat or puffing up my tissue cells. Healing the relationship I have with myself and my self image will help illuminate light into the dark parts of my soul that don't feel worthy. I will be able to see, where I don't love myself enough to have a healthy fit body. I release all self judgment, self hate and self limiting crap. I either adore my body with a few extra pounds on it or I adore my body enough to lose the weight. Losing weight is as much mental as it is physical. It's a combination of fat burning exercise, awesome

fiber scraping nutritious food, juicy self flushing liquids, self love, healing past hurts – wounds – resentments – body shame and having a desire to make it happen. If I want help letting go of the extra few pounds, healing my emotional eating, self loving myself more and the ability to be the best version of myself, then I join *Petra's Everything You Need To Know To Get Healthy & Thriving Health Pogram or her 5 Day Juice & Smoothie Cleanse*. Both will help me lose weight and lose the emotional crap that is keeping me fat in the first place.

13. I remove or reduce animal products out of my diet and lifestyle. I start to see past the illusion of the old school food pyramid, that told me I need to eat meat, dairy and eggs to survive. I realize that this food pyramid was funded by the meat, dairy and egg industry and is out dated. I recognize that meat protein, dairy and cheese actually clog my arteries, carry many cancer causing viruses, are acidic to my body, create mucous and inflammation within me and make my body sick. I recognize that dairy casein is more linked to cancer, than smoking is to lung cancer. I awaken to the intense cruelty, torture, injustice, brutality and murder of the commercial meat, dairy and egg industry. I awaken to where my meat comes from and the amount of hormones, antibiotics, GMO feed and terror that my meat is filled with. I remember that everything is energy, and my meat holds an intense amount of terror, slaughter and brutality energy within it. I research further the bovine virus that is found in most commercial meat and dairy, and how it creates cancer within my body. I educate myself by watching these movies – *Forks Over Knives, Cowspiracy, Food Matters & Food Inc.* I no longer have a disconnect to what is on my plate and what I am putting inside my body. I let go of

the crap of mainstream big corporation and government funded brainwashing and make a stand for a healthier world and for my healthier body. I see that animals are living creatures that share the planet with me and I don't need to harm or abuse them for my own selfish lifestyle.

EXERCISE 3: LETTING GO OF CRAP IN MY MIND

Letting go of crap in my mind is a hard one too. Now that I have more control over my mind, I practice cleansing here too. My mind is where old wounds from childhood, past hurts from lovers, past rejections from work, past grievances and lots more old crap is hanging out. I am carrying my mind crap with me in my life. Big bags of mind crap I lug from situation to situation. Bags of crap I carry into every new relationship. Bags of crap I bring into each new opportunity, collaboration or venture. My mind is also storing bags of crap that are a fear of the future. Crap that hasn't even happened yet and I am already clinging to bags and bags of this perceived fear that is about to happen. I feel tired because my body is bogged down with bags and bags of mind crap. So it's time to let it all go so I can be lighter and freer.

1. I brain dump all I have on my mind. I get a journal or a white board or excel document and write down everything I want to do and have to do. All my dreams. All my plans. All my to do tasks. Anything I want to create. All that I want to heal and change in my life. I get it all out and down so it is organized and no longer weighing my mind down.

2. I meditate. I sit in silence every morning and before I go to bed. I pause for a few minutes on my lunch break or as I sit at the traffic light in my car. I connect to myself. I am present. I see what old crap is weighing me down in the moment. I see what future fear is pulling me down. I am a witness to my life and to my mind. What is currently pulling at my energy? What is zapping me? What in my life and in my body needs healing?

3. On a daily basis, I practice self worth, self love and self nurturance. I work on myself. A lot. All the time. This never stops. I keep working on my connection to myself. I love and adore myself more and more. I am my own best friend. I waste no time in being the greatest happiest fullest expression of myself on this planet.

4. I do my forgiveness exercises. I purge the anger, resentment, jealousy, fear, insecurities and guilt. I open up my valve of love to flow more freely. I let go of my energetic grip on people, I release them and I release myself. I forgive and stop the mental poison flowing through my veins.

5. I look in the mirror. I say hi to myself. I tell myself I am amazing. I fall in love with myself.

6. I speak my truth. I am fully self-expressed. I stand up for my rights. I stand up for my beliefs. I do what feels right. I am kind. I follow my heart. I follow my soul. I stay in integrity with my heart. I listen to my intuition and follow my inner guidance system.

7. I take notice of the mental and verbal stories I spin about myself and others. I drop the old stories. I recreate people as fresh and new every day. I recreate myself. I no longer keep people forced into the old belief system I have about them. I don't force myself there either. I don't judge. I don't blame. I am kindness, love and compassion to others and to myself.

8. I let go of victim consciousness. I stop seeing everyone as attacking me. I stop seeing them as my aggressor. I stop thinking everyone is out to get me. I recognize everyone is a wound waiting to happen and everyone is very sensitive. I recognize I am too. I don't take anything personally. I stop thinking the universe is messing with me and I take 100% responsibility for my life.

9. I study the book, *"The Four Agreements"* and make these 4 agreements my personal values.

10. I remember that this is my dream. This life is my movie and I am dreaming it all up. I am casting roles in my film with various people. To learn my lessons. To heal my patterns. To raise my vibration. I remember I can recreate or change my movie at any time. I am the movie projector and the movie I out picture is all up to me.

11. I remember I am a vibrational being made up of love energy. The name of the game is to raise my vibration. Vibrate higher and faster. Be lighter. Be more enlightened and create more love on this planet. I heal myself and all those around me with my love energy. I have this power. Yes I am powerful!

CHAPTER 18

Victim Consciousness

NOW I DIVE DEEPER INTO MY GRIPS with victim consciousness so I can let it go within myself for good. I was taught that life is happening to me and that I don't have much control of the outcome. I should do the best with what I have and "hope" for the best. I should try to be happy with my circumstances and work hard to get ahead.

I bought into this way of thinking and I worked hard. I worked hard to conquer life. To succeed in life. To have the best life. To have a better life than my neighbor. I worked hard to compete with others and strived for the life I idolized in magazines and on TV. I worked hard. So hard in fact that I slowly burned myself out and I was not happy. The harder I worked, the unhappier I became, the more I blamed others, the more I succumbed to victim consciousness and the "poor me, it's all happening to me" same old story.

Well it's time to shake up my old way of thinking. Time to see that I was not taught to be an empowered sovereign healthy human...and it's up to me to learn this now.

WHAT I WAS NOT TAUGHT IN SCHOOL...

This life is my creation. This life is my reality. I make it what I will. Every one of my conscious or subconscious thoughts shapes my life reality. The picture I see out there, all around me is a result of my inner self. My inner thoughts, beliefs, attitudes and words I use, create my out-pictured life. My life is orchestrated by me, for me. I am slowly awakening to this knowing. My life is totally, 100% my life-out-picturing itself from the messages it receives from my heart and soul. I start really looking at and questioning what I see outside of me, so I have the clues of what I want to heal inside of me. I am in charge.

I am NOT a victim to my circumstance or to my relationships. In every moment I can choose differently. In every moment I can speak up. In every moment I can choose to love myself instead of suffering in pain. No one is doing anything to me, I am dreaming my life up so I can heal and elevate myself to the next level of donkey kong. At any time, I can ask myself, "why is this happening? What is this telling me? What is this showing me? There are no accidents. All things happen for a reason. Why did this show up in my life right now?" There are no "weird coincidences", only signs from the universe.

I WAS ALSO NOT TAUGHT THIS IN SCHOOL...

I am in charge. I can connect to the divine source of all that is for guidance. I do not need a priest or a church to connect through. I can tune in to God / Goddess on my own. I have this same power as my priest. I too am completely connected to the greater existence of consciousness on this planet and I can ask for miracles of support any time I want. All I have to do is ask. It is my birth right to have miracles enter my life upon my asking. I use the power of prayer or request miracles as I need. It is not selfish to ask for miracles daily. I am a powerful human and miracles are part of my existence.

I meditate. I silence my mind and listen to the whispers of the universe as she directs me with guidance. It might not be easy at first. I might hear all my voice chatter. I might listen to a guided meditation to ease me into the experience and can find many on YouTube. When I silence my mind and start looking within, I notice I have an inner compass inside of me. It's an inner guidance system that is speaking to me and directing me in every moment. Am I listening to it? Have I been taught to use it? Most likely I've heard it speak up a few times but I dismissed it. I thought it was 'weird' or I was too afraid to hear what it was saying, so I pretended to not hear it. This inner guidance system can help me guide the actions of my life. The more I listen and surrender to what this voice is saying, the more my life will be in alignment with my soul and heart purpose.

My life purpose and evolution is for me to become my greatest expression of myself in this lifetime. The universe wants me to express myself in to my full bloom, sing my song, dance my dance, paint my painting, create my creation, write my book, speak my poetry and express myself. The universe wants me to express myself as the most spectacular version of myself, what ever that looks like to me. That is why I am here. To become my full greatest self expression, create the most positive footprint on this planet, fall in love with myself and feel ignited by my life.

I may not choose to do it. I may not aspire to fully self-express myself. I may feel happier staying safe in my smallness. Clinging to the rocks and twigs of the running creek, afraid to let go, unsure of what might be downstream. I would rather cling to the sides. Cling to my safety and my small vision of the world. Cling to my current reality, no matter how messed up it may be. I don't like uncertainty or change. I am afraid to let go and not be in control. I am afraid of the unknown and would rather cling to my security. And that is ok. It is my choice. My life karma is up to me. I am the captain of my soul.

However, I may choose to do it, to let go and swim down the current of the creek. I trust in life unfolding. I trust the universe has my back and I am always taken care of. I trust the flow and whispers of the universe, to guide me on my life journey. I open up my ears. I open up my arms. I open up my heart. I let go. I choose empowerment and I let go of victim consciousness now and forever.

I WAS NOT TAUGHT THIS IN SCHOOL EITHER...

I am connected to all that is in the universe. I am energy. I am vibrational energy that is filling my skin body bag. This energy is moving me around. Making everything work and function. Without this energy inside of my body, I will be a dead empty skin bag. This energy inside of me vibrates. It vibrates at high or low frequencies depending on the internal out-picturing signals I am sending out in to the universe. I am a dial. I set my frequency and I broadcast. What frequency am I sending out and attracting back in? Like tuning the radio dial, what ever channel frequency I tune to will be the frequency I put out and then magnetize back in. I am a magnet. I put energy out and energy comes back in. If I want to bring in misery and suffering then I tune my vibration to this frequency (mostly unconsciously) and attract this into my life.

As I tune my frequency to beauty, bliss and joy, more and more of this vibration will be brought into my life. Music puts out a vibration too. I know the difference in my body when I listen to heavy rock metal or when I listen to spa Zen music. One vibration creates more scattered energy inside of myself and the other creates a sense of calm and peace. I am made up of energy and I am made up of water. The energy and the water inside my body skin bag vibrate by the music I play at them. All people and situations around me affect my energy. Whether subtly or unconsciously, I am constantly being vibrated.

I am vibrated by the people I surround myself with, by the shows I watch and by the words I say to myself. If I speak kindness and love to myself, I will be happier and healthier. If I speak hate and anger towards myself, I will slowly shrivel. I can either thrive or I can shrivel. I choose.

How does my energy affect other people? If I speak a low vibration nasty comment to someone, I will lower their vibration. If I speak a high vibration comment filled with kindness and love, I will lift up their vibration. I am this powerful and we are all this affected by energy. I am an empath. We all are. Most people are closed to this idea or this experience of empathy because they are not connected to their feelings or their body. We all feel emotions, we all feel each other's emotions, we all feel compassion and our hearts break when we are sad. We are empaths and we feel. We might have gotten disconnected but we are heart centered beings. I thrive when I remember this and when I live more in my heart than in my head.

I am sensitive. I am heart centered. I am a light and love warrior. I thrive in positive high vibration environments and with high vibrational beings. If I receive anything less, I have to compensate, have to lower my expectations and settle for mediocre as my heart slowly breaks knowing we are all capable of so much more. We all have the potential to be so much more. I have the potential to be so much more. This planet has the potential to be so much more. My life and my reality have the potential to be so much more.

THIS I DIDN'T LEARN IN SCHOOL EITHER...

I am a superhero. I am powerful. I am a powerful manifestor. I can awaken inside my dream and realize I am dreaming. Right now I start being awake inside my dream and I consciously start creating my life step by delicious step. I am powerful. I am empowered. To declare my own empowerment, juices me up to the next level of my evolution. It gives me full power and full accountability over my life right here, right now. No one to blame. No one to point the finger at. No one to stop me. No one to seek approval from. No one to use as an excuse any more. It's all on me. I am responsible for myself and my experience of life on this planet. This life is NOT happening to me. I am slowly thinking / feeling / dreaming up my future and then watching it come to fruition. From now on I do this consciously.

I sit and close my eyes and visualize my perfect life, my perfect body, my perfect relationship and my perfect career. I choose inside myself that this will be and that it is already so. I choose to manifest my life into existence as I want it. I don't hope it will be so, I choose it to be so. I am a powerful manifestor and I manifest my life into existence exactly how I want it. Down to the finest detail.

RIGHT NOW
RIGHT HERE
I END
VICTIM CONSCIOUSNESS
IN MY LIFE
FOREVER

...

CHAPTER 19

Power Of My Language

ONE OF THE MOST IMPORTANT TOOLS I can use to create my reality is the power of my language.

I can use the power of language to create anything to be so. If I declare it, so shall it be. I state it, the universe agrees and gives me evidence to prove me right. "I am smart" "I am dumb" both true if I declare them and my experience of life is very different based on which statement I speak. I keep declaring these 'truthful' statements and the universe's job is to agree and support me.

"I am sad" is true for me as long as I hold on to sad depressing feelings and keep listening to the depressing thoughts in my head. My thoughts create my emotions. If I keep thinking I am sad and focusing on all the reasons I am sad, then I will feel sad.

I can declare "I am happy", even if I don't feel happy yet. I start thinking happy positive thoughts and start pulling my vibration up a few levels so I vibrate lighter and it will be so. I will feel happy. I can laugh out loud for 1 min too which always helps. The more I think these happy thoughts, the more my body will respond and my emotions will start to feel happier. I am in charge of my mind and what is swirling through it.

I spin tales with the power of my language. I loop friends into my stories and create massive discussions all from the perspective of my version of truth. My story. My belief. My view. My opinion. My truth. I spin the story into existence as I speak it. I create how people perceive me. I train people how to treat me. If I feel low about myself, or afraid to speak up, then I give people permission to push up against my boundaries. If I don't value myself, I will attract people to me to show me "they don't value me either".

I watch the signs and I see these people reflecting my own internal belief systems about myself. How I speak about myself, how I speak about other people, how I speak about my life tells people a lot about me. So from now on, I think twice before I speak ill of myself. I catch myself every time I put myself down. I judge myself less. I judge other people less. I speak only kind words out of my mouth and I am aware that my words create my life. What language will I use to describe my story? Disempowering experiences or empowered ones? I get to choose.

EXERCISE: THE MOST IMPORTANT TOOLS TO EMPOWER MY LANGUAGE

1. I AM is the most valuable statement in the English language. What follows I AM is actually even more valuable and sets the tone of my truth. I am what? I am what? I am what? What am I? What do I say about me all the time? What do I keep repeating? Is there a theme? Is there an old crap story I can finally let go of? I am tired. I am bored. I am not wanted. I am not liked at work. I am not seen in my school. I am not heard by my father. I am stupid. I am forgetful. I am unlucky. I am not good at this. I am afraid. I am worried. I am sad. I am angry. I am always late. I am not good enough. I am alone. What else do I say I am? What kind of spells am I weaving with the power of my language and the power of my I AMs? How many positive I AMs am I saying? Am I using my I Am for my empowerment or my diminishment?

2. NEED is a nasty little word. I need this. I need that. I need to do this. I need to do that. I need to have that. I need to be that. I need to wear that. I need to eat that. I need to go to the gym. I need to lose weight. I need to get a check up. I need to stop smoking. I need to start drinking green smoothies. So much make wrong energy with every I NEED. It's a tightening and constricting of my body. I don't feel empowered when I NEED all over myself. I am making myself wrong in some way so I NEED to change me. I already start out in the negative when I use the word need. It comes from the energy of fear and scarcity. It comes from lack. I am missing something and so I NEED it. It is not an empowering way to inspire myself and others.

3. WANT is the empowered replacement for NEED. What about if I wanted something? I might want this or I might want that. I am powerful to make a choice. I can have both if I want or I can choose. I am in charge of my life. I am empowered. I powerfully choose my every step. I want to go the gym. I want to drink a green smoothie. Yes that is what I want. I don't need it. I want it. One is disempowered. The other is empowered. Out of all the possibilities of choices I can make in the world, I powerfully choose this one. I want it. I don't need it. I want it. I want this. I want that. I want to do this. I want to do that. I want to have that. I want to be that. I want to wear that. I want to eat that. I want to go to the gym. I want to lose weight. I want to get a check up. I want to stop smoking. I want to start drinking green smoothies. I don't need it. I want it.

4. BUT is another nasty little word. It creates limitation and puts a damper on what ever I am talking about. I try to move forward energetically and BUT just pulls me back. I make a statement and by adding the word BUT, I negate the statement. Using the word BUT in a conversation, creates the "oh no, what is she going to say next?" feeling in the other person. It's the big BUT drop. "Oh she just dropped the BUT, now what?". It is used way too commonly in my language, and yet I am unaware of the energetic vibration of this word. "I love you....BUT.....I can't come over for dinner tonight" is innocent enough yet imagine the other person listening. I say I love you and that feels good for the other person, then I drop the BUT, and they wonder, "You love me but what???!!" It creates a subtle confusion or a subconscious anxiety in someone as they wonder.... "what is she going to say next?"

5. AND is the empowered replacement for BUT. Changing my BUT to AND is a much more powerful and positive way to speak. "I love you.... AND I can't come over for dinner tonight" creates so much more peace and assurance in the other person. "I want to do business with you... BUT.... (yikes what is she going to say next?) I have to fly to Australia for 5 months" OR "I want to do business with you... AND... I have to fly to Australia for 5 months". The BUT statement is constricting, limiting and negates the first part of my sentence. The AND statement is open, moving forward and is a yes to it all. BUT creeps in to my language with other people and in my language with myself. With my new awareness for the power of words and language, I now notice how much this limiting word creeps in and I change it. I am more aware to catch my BUTs and replace them with ANDs.

6. TRY is also a nasty little word that feels innocent enough yet limits the ownership of my experiences of life. "I will try and do this" or "I will try and do that" are staments that don't make sense because there is no such action as try. "Do or do not, there is no try" as master Yoda says in Star Wars. Yet this is truth, I cannot try and do something, I can only do it or not do it. I try and pick up a box of tissues or I do not. So every time I use the word TRY, I am limiting myself and my experience of life. I am refusing to take ownership of my action of doing so I weaken outby saying try. I cannot try anything. I either do it or I do not. So I take out this limiting word out of my vocabulary and up level my reality.

7.   SHOULD is another word I take out of my vocabulary as fast as possible. How many times in a day do I should on myself? How often do I should on other people? I should do this. I should do that. You should do this. You should do that.   Much like the word need, should has a disempowering make wrong contracting energy to it. It makes me feel like I am already messing up in some way and I SHOULD fix it. Releasing my shoulds creates more freedom and empowerment in my life.

6. I stop speaking ill of people.   I stop gossiping. I stop speaking about people when they are not there. I speak kindness. I speak love. I stop spreading hate. I stop creating stress in my life and in others. Yes sometimes it feels good to hash out my issue with a friend. Sometimes I just have to rant to my friend about XYZ and how upset I feel. Yet how many friends do I tell this same story? How many people hear me speak ill of someone over and over? How many times do I really have to share this? How long do I want to keep spreading hate? Do I keep brewing about XYZ in my head? I can't stop talking about XYZ. I spread my tale to the next person I meet and the next. I keep spreading my power of black magic about XYZ and pulling other people into my situation which has nothing to do with them.

How unkind will I be to people who have wronged me? How cruel and feisty will I get? Can I keep my issues mainly to myself? Heal them and forgive them within? Can I keep my issues between me and XYZ mainly private? If I spread dark hateful energy about XYZ to other people, then they too will feel these emotions towards XYZ. They will start to feel frustration, anger and upset at XYZ even if they have no idea who or what XYZ is. I have tainted their perception with "my truth" rather than allowing them to make their own opinions. So I no longer abuse the power of my language by spreading black magic. I spread only love, not hate, out of my lips.

7. I catch every time I speak about my own experience and use the word YOU to describe me. When I speak about myself, it makes sense to use the word I. But society has programmed me to use the collective YOU word a lot. This is the ultimate way I am disempowering myself by not even owning my own experience of life. Here's an example: I've just come back from the most amazing romantic weekend with my love and I proposed to her and she said yes. I am at the office on Monday and telling my coworker about my experience.

Coworker asks: "So how was your weekend? Tell me all about it?" I say: "It was amazing. I loved every minute of it. It was a 4 hour drive out of town. YOU drive down a narrow road, and YOU wind around all these sharp corners super tight, YOUR girl is beside YOU, squealing and asking YOU to slow down. YOU arrive at the hotel. YOU get a free drink and YOU know YOU have made it to luxury. You know what I mean?"

The entire experience of my amazing weekend was put on my coworker like it was their experience instead of mine. Yes everyone uses the word YOU in this way, it's the collective, it's just how we all talk. Well staying limited to this old way of speaking will keep my experience of life small. I choose to take ownership of my experience. I choose to up level my language. I choose to take full ownership of my life and speak from the I perspective, owning, feeling and living each of my experiences fully.

People will tell me that YOU is a generic way we have been taught to speak. That it's no big deal if I use YOU or I. They are just words they will say. Bull crap! It's another way I get to be disconnected from myself. Another way I don't take full accountability of my life. Another way I don't feel my own experiences, emotions, feelings and growths that go with my own daily life.

My coworker didn't go on a romantic windy road weekend with their fiancé. I did. So I tell the same story again and this time I own it. My coworker will find my story more interesting when I come from the I perspective as it will have a different tone and energy. The I version is....

I say: "It was amazing. I loved every minute of it. It was a 4 hour drive out of town. I drove down a narrow road, and I wound around all these sharp corners super tight, my girl is beside me squealing and asking me to slow down. I arrived at the hotel. I got a free drink and I knew I have made it to luxury. You know what I mean?"

This is the most tricky power of language step to catch. Most likely I and people around me are disconnected from our experiences and our emotions. Yes everyone does talk in the form YOU and it is the norm, yet every one is also walking around quite disempowered and lost in the world. So perhaps owning my experience will help me ground into my life just a little more. What have I got to lose, but time and my life....

CHAPTER 20

I Am Grateful

WHAT AM I GRATEFUL FOR? WHAT ARE 10 things I am grateful for? What are 100 things I am grateful for? Am I counting my gratitude daily? Am I connected to my gratitude? How often am I using my gratitude muscle? Can I tune into my gratitude and tear up from the very joy I feel? Do I realize how powerful gratitude is?

For my life to be extraordinary, juicy, vibrant, spectacular and amazing, then gratitude has got to be my new attitude. What is my alternative? Grumpy, resisting, ungrateful and stingy? I choose grateful instead. I drop into deep appreciation for my existence on this planet and I become more humble to it. I let go of ego for a moment. I get really humble and grateful for my privilege to exist on this planet.

I am grateful that creation keeps breathing me. I don't have to do anything. My breath just happens automatically. While I sleep. While I drive. While I love. While I read these pages. Creation is breathing me. Breathing my skin body bag.

Up and down. In and out. Without me even giving it any thought. Without me having to count or keep timing. It is my gift for being alive on this planet. I have the gift of breath. So every morning I start my day thanking the universe for another day of breath and the privilege to walk around this spectacular planet I call home.

Gratitude helps me drop into my heart. I become more aware of all the little moving pieces that make up my world and I express thank you. I am thankful for my bed. I am thankful for having clothes. I am thankful for clean drinking water. I am thankful for food to eat. I am thankful for my cell phone and for the people and resources it took to create it. Thank you to my credit card company for letting me swipe my plastic and buy things. Thank you. Thank you to the almond farmers for my almond milk and thank you to the coffee farmers for my coffee. Thank you to the warm sun and to the earth for growing my food so full of nutrition, life force and vibration to feed me. Thank you to my mind for being so open and smart. Thank you to my heart for searching for a brighter, lighter, happier, more peaceful way for me to live in the world. Thank you to my body for carrying me around. Thank you..... Thank you..... Thank you....

I drop into my heart as much as possible while I am counting my gratitude. I drop into my heart as much as possible while I am living life too. Scientists have now proven that my heart is my 2nd brain, which they say is actually more powerful in making choices and leading my life than the one in my head. Following the calls of my heart will not lead me astray. Leading my life from my head, I can sometimes become too egoic and get myself in trouble. Dropping back into my heart, drops my ego and brings more love to any situation.

I can use my heart to create a lot of power in my life. Living in my heart is a very powerful place for me to be. I show up as more love than those around me. Being more in my heart allows me to hold space for those suffering. I shine my light bright. I am here to serve. I am here to help people, my family and the world in some way. I am able to raise the vibration of any situation to be lighter just by being me. I am not seeking love from others. I am full of love for myself. I charge up my own love tank and give love to others around me. All those around me need love too. And they need it much more desperately than me. They are starving for love, acknowledgement and appreciation. They too didn't receive it from their parents or their teachers. And they don't know YET how to give it to themselves. They don't know YET that they have this power. They don't YET have a copy of this book to remind them (wink wink). I can show up as a bigger love energy in their life. I can give more love and acknowledgement to them. I can guide them towards loving themselves much more. I can help them fill their own self love tank so they start overflowing too. Of course all this AFTER I have mastered it on myself first.

EXERCISE: COUNTING GRATITUDE

This exercise is one of the fastest ways out of my misery, self loathing, fear and insecurity. It works extra magical when I say it out loud. I keep count using my fingers. I do this exercise even when I don't feel like doing it. I do this exercise even when I barely believe it. I do it even when I am feeling miserable on the inside. I still DO IT!

1. I wake up every morning and say out loud 10 things I am grateful for.

2. I do it daily till forever...

I AM GRATEFUL

CHAPTER 21

I Be Love

BE LOVE! THAT'S IT! I BE LOVE in every situation. I BE LOVE in every moment. I BE LOVE in every interaction with myself. I BE LOVE in every interaction with my lover, my kids, my parents, my neighbors, my bus driver, my fast food take out clerk (oh note to myself: stop eating fast food that is poisoning my body with preservatives, chemicals and not real food ingredients and I choose making a daily morning green smoothies instead.) I BE LOVE to myself.

I can become a love so big that it might feel unimaginable to me right now. I am willing to go there. I am willing to expand my heart. I am willing to rise above my smallness. I am willing to be GREAT and to be LOVE for those around me who are so desperately seeking some taste of it. I remember I can generate my own sense of love and self worth. I don't need to find someone to feed me. I remember I am the source of the love glow inside of me. I can generate it within myself with or without a partner.

EXERCISE: HARNESSING THE POWER OF BE LOVE

1. I expand my ability to love. I forgive. I release. I heal past wounds. I let go of expectations. I release judgments. I begin being more kind. I begin being more compassionate. I see my brothers and sisters like me, amazing and faulty at the same time. I let go of judgment. I let go of segregation. I let go of my rigidity. I let go of being one way and doing it one way. I see a new perspective. I expand. I am expansive. I forgive people in every moment. I observe more than I judge. I don't judge. I am love. Big love. I am a safe place for others to rest.

2. I see no one as misbehaving. I see everyone as doing the best they can. No one is purposely trying to hurt me. I am willing to see that everyone makes mistakes. I speak up if I feel hurt. I speak my feelings to create a healing rather than a blow out fight. I don't use the energy of big fights to finally speak my truth. I speak my truth in peace, centeredness and love. I start switching my mind perspective and seeing my partner as on my side rather than my battle partner. I approach my partner with a situation or a hurt for help to heal, rather than an attack that creates war. If we are constantly attacking each other, it cannot create a trustworthy relationship. If I always feel attacked by my partner, then I am constantly living in turmoil. Instead I see my partner as a wounded - scared - trying - the - best - they - can - person, just like me and we work on things together, instead of against each other. We are on the same team to help and heal each other.

3. I take nothing personally. No one is ever really that focused on me, that they are making everything about me. Everyone is having their own experience of life. I might trigger some old wound or some pain inside someone and they react and get upset at me, but it's still what ever is actually going on inside them. I don't have ultimate control to create anger or frustration or jealousy inside anyone. They either have that pain or wound or insecurity and I trigger them into feeling it. Why? So they can heal it of course. As an example: If I announce my promotion to my coworker and she gets nasty on me, I can take it personally or I can understand that I probably triggered something inside of her. Perhaps she was hoping for a promotion herself and has been waiting a long time. Perhaps she is frustrated. Perhaps she feels rejected. So when I tell her my great news, it triggers her insecurities and she barfs all her annoyance on me. It is not personal although it feels like it in the moment.

4. I BE LOVE to everyone I meet. I hold bigger space. I raise my vibration. I fill my love tank first. I stay empowered. I drop victim consciousness. I am a warrior on this planet. I shine bright. I keep my vibration high. I inspire others. I help people. I am a good person. I am kind. I help the planet. I help humanity. I create a better world for the next generation. I create a world that is much safer, happier, healthier, more sovereign and more full of LOVE LOVE LOVE LOVE LOVE!

5. I BE LOVE to myself. I take care of my body and I learn to heal my darker emotions, insecurities, not enoughness, jealousy, anger and resentment. When I feel these emotions bubble up to the surface, I want to scream. I want to run. I cry and it hurts. I feel the pain inside my body. I feel it in order to heal

it. I don't ignore it and hope it goes away or numb myself out so I don't have to face it. No. I feel it. I get in touch with it. I forgive myself. I release the pain. I give myself assurance and self love. I remember I am amazing, miraculous, fabulous and divine! And I ask for a miracle of healing, strength, empowerment and laughter as soon as possible.

EXERCISE: ACKNOWLEDGING SOMEONE

Giving someone praise, acknowledgement, a compliment and gratitude are amazing ways I BE LOVE in my life. I am willing to see someone and feel comfortable enough to acknowledge them. The more I am willing to give praise to another, the more my own desire for praise is fulfilled. The more empowered I am as a super human on this planet, the more I lift someone's spirit with the power of my words.

1. I tap into my heart. I get into my heart. I breathe into my heart.

2. I think of the gratitude I have for this person. I think of who they are. What they mean to me. How they inspire me. What they represent for the world. How beautiful they are. How huge their heart is.

3. I speak my truth. I stay kind and compassionate. I listen to my higher intelligence to find the words to say if I am unsure.

4. If I am still unsure how to acknowledge someone or the words to use, I think, what I would like to be acknowledged for? What words would I like to hear? We are all mirrors for each other. When I see your greatness I know it is my greatness too or the greatness I am aspiring too. I look at all the traits I admire and aspire to in this person. I let them know they are amazing. I tell them they matter. I tell them I see them and I appreciate them. I let them know I like how they show up in the world and I like their energy. I acknowledge them for being a great parent and doing brave work in the world. I look at their traits. Their beliefs. Their ways of showing up. Their integrity. Their bravery. Their courage. Their lifestyle. Their vitality. Their energy. Their character. I BE LOVE by speaking uplifting words to another.

5. I build my muscle of acknowledgement for others and I build my muscle of asking for acknowledgment from others. It is not selfish to ask for recognition or praise. It is self full. I fill my own love tank and I ask others to help me fill it. I am worthy.

I BE LOVE
IN EVERY MOMENT
WITH EVERY PERSON
I BE LOVE

...

I BE LOVE
IN EVERY MOMENT
WITH MYSELF
I BE LOVE

CHAPTER 22

Loving & Hating Connection

I WANT CONNECTION. I WANT TO BE SEEN and heard by others. I want to be appreciated, loved and seen as a valuable member of my family, my community and my tribe.

Yet for how much I desire connection, I am actually super afraid of it. Opening myself up fully to another human being is terrifying. Opening myself up to many human beings is even more terrifying. Allowing all of myself to be vulnerable and to be seen is frightening. So I have this internal battle of wanting to be seen and yet hiding myself at the same time.

Most of us are quite lonely in relationships and families even when we have tons of people around. Most of us don't feel seen or heard by those that matter most. We feel inauthentic in our relationships and feel separate in our loving intimate loverships.

My deepest desire for connection usually goes unmet and I am left hurt and searching for other ways to feel fulfilled. Firstly, I am walking around with NOT ENOUGH syndrome, taking everything personally and feeling hurt by everyone all the time. Secondly, I don't really know how to reach out and connect with someone. I am secretly afraid of deep intimate connection with my spouse, parents and friends. I avoid eye contact for some fear of being seen too closely. I sit and watch TV as together time. I play with my cell phone instead of talking and looking into my partner's eyes.

What am I so afraid of? Afraid that the other will see my flaws? My imperfections? My not so good stuff? Maybe if they see it, they won't like me anymore. Maybe if they see it, I too will have to see it and face myself. Urgh that sounds scary. Facing myself and looking at myself. Making changes. Choosing higher vibration thoughts and letting go of the old yucky stuff that no longer serves me. Sounds like too much work.

Sometimes I don't want to look. I would rather distract myself, get drunk or get high. I would rather leave the relationship or watch lots of TV to avoid the connection that I am feeling forced into. I would rather be distracted so I don't have to look at myself. Distracted so I don't have to look at all the bull crap stuff I have been telling myself for years to validate my excuses for not living life fully. Can I keep living an inauthentic dull life pretending to be happy when I am crying in pain and suffering on the inside? Ok, maybe I'm not crying in pain, that might sound too harsh. I'm happy. It's all good. I make the best of it. I feel content. I can put on a good smile.

But is my happiness and big smile surface based and what I show to the outside world? Is there suffering and pain on the inside? In the depths of my heart and soul, am I suffering?

If so, I fix it.

What is my biggest fear about intimacy and connection anyway? That I will not be loved back? That I will not be accepted and loved for who I am? That I will be reminded of my not enoughness? That I will give my heart to someone and be hurt? That I will not be seen, heard or understood? That I will feel lonely inside my relationship? Yes all these things can happen and as I build my muscle of self love, self adoration and self acceptance, other's opinions will no longer affect me with so much charge. I will be free.

In the past, I have put too much attention on the outside world and all the people in it. Their opinions matter so much to me. Their power of acceptance or their power of rejection can feel like life or death for me. I am addicted to external validation. It's no wonder. I come from a tribal mentality. My ancestors lived in tribes and being part of a tribe meant survival. If I was ostracized by the tribe and cast out on my own, I would likely die. I would be eaten by some big animal or killed by the enemy tribe. Back then, being alone was not safe for my survival and this feeling is ingrained in my bones. I like to belong. I like to be part of something or someone. I like the safety and community of a tribe. I am meant to live in community for my greatest thrival on this planet. Yet I no longer need community for survival, now I want it to flourish, feel supported, have fun and thrive with my likeminded tribe.

I want to belong. I want others to like me. I want to be accepted. I truly want to live and be in community. I want people around me, supporting me, helping me. Raising our kids together and creating a garden together. Having people around who understand and support me, takes some of the pressure off life and living. I want the love, the family, the fun and the laughs. I want to feel at peace and I want to be happy. I want my family to be healthy and safe. I want to love myself. I want to accept myself. I want to see my own greatness. I want to feel happier and be kinder to those around me. I want more connection, more acceptance and more adoration in my life. I want to feel joy and peace when I wake up everyday.

So let's have it. I truly want it. Might be a bit afraid of it. But I am ready.

I feel the fear and do it anyway. I have suffered in mediocrity long enough so I am ready to change all my wants into action. I am ready to fully actualize my life, my health and my love life! I am ready. I am good enough. I am brave. I can do anything. The universe loves me and is always conspiring for my greatness. I open my heart and love more fully. I am kinder to people. I am kinder to myself. I create more love where ever I go. I am committed to love, creating love and bringing peace. I practice love and peace. I practice acceptance, non-irritation, forgiveness, kindness and connection. I want love around me. I am not afraid of love. I receive more love into my life. Love is safe. I am surrounded by love all the time. I am a love being. I radiate love. I can give someone love just by thinking of them. I can give love with one look. I can give love with a touch or hand gesture. I can send my love to the other side of the world. I can give love freely to everyone I know because I have an infinite amount. It will never run out and never go away. So I give... give... give love and create connection.

Before reading this book, I would have said "I don't let people into my heart zone or I don't let them in easily or I don't let them in often". Now knowing how powerful I am... how great I am... how enough I am... and how much I truly desire love and connection.... Now I say YES to more and more heart opening practices as my life continues. I only have this one life to live, so I make it extraordinary. I live my life to the fullest and get to experience the spectrum of all life has to offer. I keep my heart open. I know that is hard to do sometimes or all the time. But what choice do I have? Walk around life with a closed, shriveled, self loathing, depressed, unworthy unloved heart? No thanks, that sounds terrible!

So I say yes! Yes to a happier life. Yes to a healthier life. Yes to a more loving and loveable life. Yes to a kinder, more peaceful life. It's starts with me. I say yes to these tools. I say yes to these practices. I do the exercises. I open up. I raise my own vibration. I inspire others to do the same. I shine my light brighter and feel happier inside.

EXERCISE: CREATING MORE CONNECTION

I do this exercise with everyone in my family. I do this with my friends. I do this with my partner. Even if it feels weird. Even if it feels awkward. Even if I am embarrassed. Even if I cry. Even if it brings up fears, wounds and hurts. This is my healing. I allow myself to be seen and I allow myself to fully see another. I feel the fear and do it anyway. Through the fear is connection and a huge hug!

1. I sit across from the person I am connecting with. We are close, a few feet apart.

2. I set my smart phone timer to 11 min. I start the timer. (maybe I start with 3 min in the beginning)

3. We sit in silence, looking at each other for 11 min.

4. I look into their eyes. They look into mine. I allow myself to be seen. To be really, really seen. Sometimes for the first time in my life. I might get teary. I might start crying. I might not know what to do.

5. There are no hand gestures, no lip synching words and no horsing around. We simply sit looking into each other's eyes. I am fully present with this person, with nothing to distract me. I am creating intimacy and connection. We are getting into each other's "heart centered" zone.

6. We breathe. We allow. We hug and are grateful for the intimacy healing we have both experienced.

CHAPTER 23

Love Relationships

WANT LOVE YET I CAN SPEND A LOT of time pushing it away. I want love yet I am secretly afraid of it. I seek someone to love and adore me yet at the core I likely feel unloveable. I want someone to finally see me yet I am afraid to be fully seen. To be fully seen means they might see my flaws and insecurities too, so I spend a lot of energy in the beginning, pretending to be perfect and have it all together. I want to be close with someone, yet true intimacy and vulnerability makes me nervous.

So I usually play safe, don't open up too much, keep my heart guarded slightly and not really give all of myself, all in the game of wanting love. I am afraid to be hurt, to be abandoned, to stop being chosen and to experience love leaving me. So I don't fully surrender or allow myself to be fully vulnerable as a way to protect my heart from the possible pain. I want love yet all my past pains, heart aches and unsuccessful loverships have put a layer of guard on my heart.

Can I let this guard go? Can I start fresh? Can I fully open with no expectations, no future dooms, no insecurities and no more chains on my heart? Can I love from a confident, secure and empowered place? Can I let myself be loveable? Can I let myself be totally adored, worshipped, appreciated, seen and respected? With no fears, no pulling back, no masks, no hiding and no manipulated guarding? Can I let myself be loved?

Sometimes I seek love, not even for a relationship but for my own personal validation. I seek someone to tell me I am great and amazing because I don't tell myself. I need someone to acknowledge me and to validate my worth. I think if I have someone loving me, then I must be worthy. I think I need a partner to finally see myself, to validate my beauty, magnificence and self worth. So I seek someone to see me because I don't see myself. To truly have the love relationship in my life I seek, I must start with my own self love relationship first. I cannot truly love another or allow myself to be truly loved, if I don't love myself. An external love relationship that is not based in my own self love, is usually inauthentic, guarded and insecure. I will always be looking to the other person to validate my worth if I don't believe I am worthy. I will always be giving someone else my personal power and although I may look like I have it all together on the surface, internally I will be struggling. Loving and adoring myself and having a lovership with myself first is the key to any successful relationship I want. Choosing myself and seeing my own amazingness is where true love starts. My own true worship is the foundation for finding the authentic heart expanding, soul completing and bed shaking love I seek. I have to be my own greatest lover, to receive authentic and real love in my life.

After I find the love relationship, my personal internal work will continue if I want to keep it. I was not taught relationships and creating healthy relationships in school. Most likely my parents were not the greatest examples of how to maneuver in love. From movies and tv shows, I have been brainwashed to believe that I will find love and live happily ever after. No one taught me that relationships will bring up my biggest insecurities and my most painful wounds. Relationships will bring up my unresolved mommy or daddy issues that are looking to be healed. My partner may start out looking like my perfect ally and then morph into my biggest enemy. So with this new found conscious awareness, I can step into relationships with more power and knowing. I can recognize that everything is my personal journey of self worth and self love. I can step into a lovership knowing a certain pattern may emerge and I can work on healing myself and supporting my partner to heal themselves too. We are a team and I do my best to remember this even though the following pattern may start to unfold....

I find my love and we are enamored with each other. We see each other as Saints and the Most Amazing Beings ever. I feel super blessed to be together and see the other just like me. I relish in all the ways we are similar and all the things we have in common. We are so perfect for each other. We are destined. It's unbelievable how we have come together. I am in love. My mate is in love. Life is good! We are in the honeymoon stage of our relationship.

Usually over time and piled up wounds, we move out of this honeymoon stage into the battle stage.

If we are both awake, aware and conscious then we can stay in the honeymoon stage forever. If we are pretty whole and healed on the inside then we really don't need to battle each other looking for our own personal healing. We can keep loving and supporting each other. Being each other's loves and best friends. Being each other's allies and being on the same team. This is ideal, to stay in kindness and love. I want the love to last. I want the good feeling to stay feeling good. I want peace and I want to be loved and accepted. I want this deep connected open love.

But some of us, without knowing how or understanding why, will slip into the battle stage. This starts where one of us sees more fault, than good in the other and begins complaining about it. I start seeing the lack of potential in my partner. The weakness. The laziness. The inabilities. Maybe I no longer find them sexy. Maybe I've lost respect. Maybe I've let the crap pile up for too long, that war and fighting is where we keep going.

In this stage we stop seeing each other as the same and start focusing on each other's differences. Big differences all of a sudden. I feel defensive and need to defend myself and my heart. I feel like my partner is out for my throat and I don't know when they will strike. Life can feel peaceful and all of a sudden my partner snaps, screams, get agitated and loses it. I feel confused, hurt and want to run far away. And so my relationship continues.

How long we stay in battle zone stage is really up to us. Most couples stay here for their whole lives. I do my best to move my relationship out of this battle stage to create peace and happiness in our life. I move my relationship to the next stage of respect, love, gratitude and reverence.

To move out of the battle stage, my relationship has to alchemize. We either separate and break up or we move to respect, love, gratitude and reverence. The latter is a very elevated way of being in a relationship. It is where I see my love as my friend and partner, even when I perceive they said something hurtful to me. We are on the same side. Always. A solid powerful team. We do not turn on each other. Why would I turn on my best friend? We work on our relationship, like we work on a garden. We water it. Weed it. Fertilize it. Admire it. Eat from it. Appreciate it. My relationship is a place for my growth, expansion and a support system to fulfill all my dreams. My partner helps me fluff up my wings to fly as high as I dare.

We do things together. We take classes together. We practice being in loving kindness together. We practice listening to each other. We practice appreciating each other. We practice loving each other bigger than we have ever loved anything or anyone before. We keep loving bigger. We are a power couple. We come together. Create sacredness and reverence together. Pray for our dreams together. Ask for miracles together. Create more magic by the power of our two. This is this next stage of respect, love, gratitude and reverence.

EXERCISE: CREATING HEALTHY RELATIONSHIPS

1. In order to have a healthy relationship, we have to sit down and heal all old wounds between us. Bring them up, without heat, and ask my partner to apologize and repair the tear. We must mend all the tears of our relationship if we expect it to continue after the battle zone stage. During this process, I may want to express my deepest love and eternal devotion for my partner and our union or I may start completing this relationship amicably and looking at separating ways. Either path, our old wounds have to be healed for a real, truthful and trustworthy relationship to continue or a true friendship to emerge out of this union.

2. We tell each other what we love and appreciate about each other. It's very important to balance the ill unkind words spoken in the past with words of love, adoration and respect.

3. We count our gratitude about each other. What we are we grateful for in the other? We appreciate our differences. We are both miraculous individuals who appreciate each other, not judge each other.

4. We find our common vision and create something together. A business. A project. A recipe. A dinner party. Music. Art. A new super food or a super dessert. Some form of collaboration and co-creation. Over and over and over again. To create a deep solid relationship, we have to be able to collaborate and co-create life together in peace, fun, harmony, joy, abundance and grace.

5. The evolution of our planet is moving away from the masculine influence of the past and moving into the feminine way of the future. It is time to worship the feminine entity. This world, for far too long has been run by the masculine energy of take, rape and pillage with mass destruction and no care for repair. It is time for the feminine energy of love, balance, compassion and grace. It is happening already, the energy of the world is shifting. Men and Women have both the feminine and masculine energies within. Loving and honoring both, creates perfect balance and harmony within us all.

The more women awaken to their power and their long forgotten stewardship of this planet, the temples, their families and their own lives - the faster our world evolution will occur. The faster men get behind their women and stand by their side as the masculine protection for the Divine All Mighty Universal Feminine Energy – the faster humanity will be healed.

Men (and women), it's time to awaken to our appreciation of the feminine. I close my eyes and breathe into the appreciation and gratitude for my mother and my sisters. I connect to being birthed and created inside the womb of the feminine divine universal energy. Maybe I hold a lot of pain here and need to forgive and release. It's hard to have a positive relationship with the love of my life when I am hanging on to old hurts from my mother and holding on to blocks towards the feminine. I close my eyes and appreciate the beauty of mother nature, the feminine forever changing and constantly creating magnificent Universe and the feminine cycles of life always unfolding. I close my eyes and appreciate the feminine goddess energy. I appreciate the multi dimensional and multi layered personality of a woman. Instead of scolding and stating "women are crazy", I let myself explore the layers, dimensions and intricacies of a woman with wonder and curiosity. Women are very intriguing and fascinating. I appreciate the inner power that a woman has to offer. She is able to expand her body and carry a baby in creation. She has super powers. Her intuition is strong. Much more fine tuned than a man's. I appreciate her. She has 14 times more energy around her body than a man, so she can pick up signals stronger, be more in tune with the universe around her and be able to multi task everything at the very same time. I appreciate this magical creature called woman.

Men, our admiration and appreciation of our woman is what makes the relationship flourish. A woman is already there for love. It is man who is usually resisting and fighting his way to the place he actually wants to be more than anything. To be in the bosom of the feminine goddess energy, being nurtured, rubbed, stroked, kissed and adored. Men resist love more than women. Men usually pull away from a loving situation first. Men want love but fear it at the same time. They fear losing their autonomy, independence and manhood.

Men, we are more powerful than we think in creating healthy loving kind relationships. Usually the energy comes from us. When our woman feels our love, our commitment, our devotion, our respect, our reverence, our adoration and worship, she can fully relax into our masculine energy and fully flourish as the powerful woman creatrix that she is.

Yes Men, we are that powerful! Men, also a woman is the barometer of us and our relationship. She can sense when we are on purpose or full of crap. She can sense when we are coming from our highest truth or bull crapping ourselves and others. Instead of yelling at her and getting upset when she asks us to face our own integrity, manhood or truth, we can let go of ego and become grateful to have her bring us back to our highest selves. Instead of letting us swim around in our bull crap and playing small, our woman brings us back to our inner truth. Our woman can help us become more aware and connected to the electric energy between the two of us. We can start to breathe together and witness how quickly our relationship transforms.

Ideally two lovers come together to inspire each other and move mountains together. Unfortunately many of us are in lovership fighting for our survival and crawl out bruised and tattered. Lovership is two people on the same side, on the same team, witnessing each other's wounds and pain bodies as they come up and supporting each other in the healing. There is no blame or projections. Each person sees the other as a mirror. Using the partnership to learn about ourselves and noticing where further internal healing needs to happen. Lovers put their dreams on the agenda and discuss ways to support these dreams in coming true. Lovers use their language and energy for collaboration and co-creation. Not much time is wasted watching useless TV, when there is much to create, do and be in this world. Our partner helps us get there. This partnership is one of support, listening, hearing, lifting up, co-creating, fun and awakening to a conscious kind heart centered union without any masks or limitations.

Men appreciate your women! Women appreciate your men!

WHAT I WAS NOT TAUGHT IN SCHOOL ABOUT RELATIONSHIPS

Relationships are actually the fastest accelerators to have my childhood wounds and insecurities come to the surface. I meet someone and think I have fallen in love. Very quickly I am shocked that all these issues, insecurities, wounds and pains start emerging to the surface. I no longer feel as safe in the arms of my love, as my childhood wounds are disguised as issues with my lover. These old pain bodies are disguised as new situations my partner is doing to me, acting towards me or aggressing on me. It is inevitable that over time my partner will take on the traits of my mother or my father. I will feel like a small child again getting reprimanded. Not being seen. Not being heard. Not mattering. Not being loved enough or feel what ever child hood issue I had growing up that might still live dormant inside of me today.

In school I should have been told, "get ready your partner will start acting like your father and you will feel triggered and think it's their fault, but it's all actually happening for you so you can heal your father issues. Or get ready your partner will resemble actions of your mother and how she treated you. You will feel shamed, scolded, nagged and disapproved of so you can heal your mother issues. This is nothing to be afraid of, it's totally normal and part of the human experience and now you are informed and ready for it. You are coming to a relationship to heal your wounds and issues. You are to heal any lack or insecurity that is preventing you from being your greatest expression of yourself on this planet and your partner will help you bring up all your smallness crap."

Instead I was taught nothing of relationships and sent on my way to go mate, have babies and live "happily ever after" with absolutely no rules or guidelines for my success.

Now can I remember all this as I am falling in love? Can I pull back and witness the wounds that keep playing out in my life and the ones that feel the most painful? Can I see where a healing is needed of my own past and the past of my partner?

I am now more empowered with more relationship knowledge and I am better prepared for potential drama and disruption of love in my relationship. It will not be easy at times. My partner's frustration might sneak up on me. It might feel personal. It might feel like a real attack. It will hurt. Can I team up with my partner and awaken within our dream? Can I see the pain we are both causing each other unnecessarily? Can we heal our own wounds? Can we be on the same team? Can we help each other to do this? Can we help each other become the greatest version of ourselves possible?

This is true partnership.

EXERCISE: USING THE 5 LOVE LANGUAGES

This book "*The 5 Love Languages*" and its concepts help me create more understanding, clarity, love and acceptance in my relationship. The book says we all speak and hear love in 5 various ways. Not all of us view and witness love in the same way. Usually the way I like to receive love is how I will give it. I think if it feels like love for me, it will feel like love for my partner. The problem lies in my partner having a different love language than me and then maybe they don't feel loved.

I can give as much touchy loving energy till I am exhausted and feel totally confused when my partner is complaining that they don't feel loved. If my partner's love language is words of affirmation then I can see that touching them and cuddling them will not be enough for them to feel loved. I love learning about my own love language, my partner's love language and my family's. I make an effort to give love to people in the love language they speak and I make an effort to request love in the language that I speak.

First I learn what my own love language is, so I can give this love to myself and be able to communicate my love language to my partner. I learn more here www.5lovelanguages.com

The 5 Love Languages Are:
1 Words of affirmation
2 Spending quality time
3 Gifts
4 Acts of service
5 Touch & affection

CHAPTER 24

I Am Grounded

D O I KNOW HOW TO GROUND into my body? Do I know how to ground into the earth? Grounding will help anchor my energy down and help me make choices from a much more secure, solid and rooted place. Grounding helps me create energetic roots into the earth and like a tree that is deeply grounded into the earth, it takes a lot to knock me over. That is how I want to be, more and more grounded to the earth and to myself just like a tree.

Sometimes I get stuff thrown at me. A million things all at the same time. Which one do I tackle first? Which one is important? How can I handle all this being thrown my way? I can learn how to ground my body, and my life tasks and choices become easier. I get grounded and centered with my imaginary roots rooted firmly into the earth and I act, speak, choose, interact from this empowered calmer place. The earth has got my back, I can use its power and tap into its energetic field.

EXERCISE: GROUNDING MYSELF WITH A GROUNDING CHORD

I can use this grounding technique before I start my day, before I host a meeting, perform a speech, go on my first date, go on a job interview or do my first live Facebook feed. I ground in and use the energy of the earth to empower and heal me.

1. I sit on a chair with my feet on the ground. I close my eyes.

2. I imagine a chord of energy coming from the base of my spine (my bum area, my first chakra). The chord is made from anything I choose. Rope. Glass. Metal. A stream of water. Tree roots. The grounding chord goes through my chair, into the floor and into the earth. Through all the layers of rock and dirt. Through all the sediment. Right in to the molten lava at the center of the earth.

3. I hook my imaginary grounding chord with a big hook into the molten lava at the center. I give it a tug. I make sure the chord is tight. I imagine this chord hooking in, till I feel tethered to the center of the earth.

4. I take a few deep breaths in and out. With my in breath, I gather up all the negativity that is inside of me and with the out breath I flush the negativity down my grounding chord to be burned up by the molten lava at the center. I vacuum or flush my negative, self limiting and self loathing crap out. I keep doing this till I feel lighter, clearer and more spacious inside.

5. With all this new energetic space within me, I empower myself with powerful words and statements to fill myself up. I am awesome. I got this. I'll ace this test. I am so smart. I've got this job. I am so amazing. I am powerful. I am beautiful. I am confident. I am brave. I am fabulous. I am strong.

EXERCISE: GROUNDING MYSELF WITH MY FEET

I can also use the earth to ground and cleanse my toxins and release the electro magnetic frequencies (EMF – from cell phones, wireless devices, cell towers, internet towers, computers, stereos, electric appliances, etc) that affect my body all the time. The earth is my friend and can help me in my healing and cleansing journey.

1. I take off my shoes. I walk on the earth barefoot as much as possible. I was never designed to have rubber souls between me and the energy of the earth. I was designed to walk barefoot. When I do, the earth responds and cleanses me, grounds me, purifies me and creates a deeper sense of peace within me. I stand with my feet firmly planted on the earth. I root my imaginary feet roots into the earth and know she has got me. I lay naked on the earth and allow her to take away all my body aches, pains and pollutants.

2. I walk on grass as much as possible. I walk on dirt. I walk on sand. I get the dirt and the sand between my toes. I relax my body into the earth and I allow her to hold me. I give her all my problems, all my woes, all my issues and ask her to take them off of me. I imagine the earth's magnetic energy, magnetizing

and rebalancing my body on a structural and energetic level.   I become more and more reconnected to the earth.

3. I soak in the ocean, lakes, rivers, creeks and waterfalls as often as possible. I cleanse my body with nature's water. The energy and cleansing power of the water will cleanse, heal and ground me. Water is flowing and healing. I use it to purify my body on the outside and of course I drink spring water and purify on the inside. I have baths as much as possible full of healing essential oils, Epsom salts, Himalayan salt, baking soda, clay and other earth elements that infuse into my skin and relax all my muscles. I seek out natural hot springs and thermal swimming pools as much as possible, so my body can soak in all the medicine from these healing waters. I swim in the ocean and absorb the magnesium (salt) into my skin. Magnesium is needed for every body and nerve function inside my body. It is the spark of life for my body to function fully optimally. I let my skin drink it up.

CHAPTER 25

I Get Spiritual
& Sacred

A M I SPIRITUAL? AM I AWAKENED? AM I conscious? Am I sacred? What do all these terminologies mean anyway? They all represent a state of attainment that is a higher vibration. I can sense there is more peace and Zen there. I want to go there. I want more sacred in my life. What does spiritual and sacred mean to me? It might mean something different to me than to someone else. For the author Petra, sacred means seeing life as more and more magical; More and more synchronistic; More and more of an interesting beautiful enfoldment to witness and receive the gifts the universe brings; and more and more connection to it all; More reverance, appreciation, prayer, gratitude, honor, love and kindness towards ourselves, all humans and all living creatures.

EXERCISE: CREATING MORE SACRED IN MY LIFE

1. Sacred and spiritual don't mean religious. I can be spiritual and not be religious. I can believe in a higher power of creation but not have to label it. A higher power I can connect to, with or without a priest or church. I am a God / Goddesses walking on this planet. This world can be my heaven right now or it can be my hell. I get to choose. I create my life. I am a creator. I create my reality into being. I can create good. I can create evil. In every moment I get to choose.

2. I add prayer into my life. I don't have to be religious to pray and ask for a miracle. It is my birthright to ask for miracles. The universe loves to dish them out and all I have to do is ask. I close my eyes. Talk to some higher power outside of me or inside me and I ask for miracles.

I can pray to a God or a Goddess. I can pray to the Infinite Magnificent Universe. I can pray to Momma Nature. I can pray to who ever and what ever feels right to me. No one can dictate my personal connection time to a higher power. I have free will. Adding prayer into my life, helps make my life be more sacred. Prayer helps remind me that I am not alone. I can ask for help. I can ask for miracles. The universe has my back and will answer my requests.

What if I don't know how to pray? Well I can't do it wrong. I just close my eyes and talk. I ask for help. I ask for guidance. I ask for clarity. I ask for wisdom. I ask to be in the right place at the right time. I ask to meet all the right people. I ask to be more of service. I ask how can I serve? I give thanks.

3. I give thanks. I count 10 things I am grateful for every morning. Even when I am feeling miserable and am not feeling grateful for anything, I count anyway. Gratitude is the fastest way to my new happier attitude. It's the fastest way to drop in to my heart. I become more present. I start witnessing more magic in my life. I stop focusing on my lack and start seeing all the abundance I have. I focus my attention on the abundance bucket, rather than the scarcity bucket.

4. I create an altar. An altar is a place where I put special things. I light candles there. I display special photos. My keep sakes. My crystal gems. My stones. My shells and special rocks. My love letters. My new business card or aspiring best seller book. I go there to tune in and to remember. It's where I can go to pray or meditate. It's where I put all that is meaningful and special to me. My altar is a special sacred place that connects me to myself, my divinity and my power. It is a focal point for my prayer and gratitude energy.

5. I go to sacred and heart centered events within my community. Music is prayer. I can go and sing, dance and be with like minded people. I can be with my tribe. Feels so good to find my tribe. Festivals. Musical concerts. Ecstatic dances. Meditation nights. Singing circles. Metaphysical talks. Consciousness seminars. All these places can help me step deeper into my power and my brightest super human state. I love being part of the convergence of like minded people who are interested in growth, expansion and owning their own reality. I find support here and a place to lift up my spirit.

6. I remember my own power. I am a creator on this planet able to create anything. I set my mind, heart and vision to what I want to create. I am powerful. I can use my words and actions to heal or to harm. I can manifest my dreams by electrically putting myself into the very vibration of what I want to manifest and attracting it to myself like a magnet. With TOTAL sureness and certainty, that it is already so.

I AM POWERFUL

CHAPTER 26

I Am A Whole Being

EXIST AS A WHOLE. I CANNOT GO to the doctor and treat my eczema as one solitary itchy patch on my elbow. A doctor can't give me cream and expect the problem to be solved. I am a whole being and that eczema stems most likely from my gut and somewhere in my mind too. My cancer is not just there to be poisoned, burned and cut out. I am a whole being. That cancer was created by my mind, my heart, my soul, my unresolved wounds, insecurities, pains and toxicity in my body. Cutting it out will only cut out the external visual of the cancer. What about all the stuff behind the scenes that the doctor isn't looking at nor asking me about that? A lot of factors could have caused my cancer. The medical field does not look for the root cause or look for the prevention. It just focuses on the evil cancer that came and attacked me out of nowhere and now we have to fry it!

Everything is part of everything. I have a fight with my boyfriend and I release him from my being. The next day I develop a yeast infection and can't have sex. The body is externally signaling what my mind has already decided.

For fun and some insight, I can look up body illnesses and the metaphysical spiritual meaning they might have by Louise Hay at

www.alchemyofhealing.com/causes-of-symptoms-according-to-louise-hay

I am connected to all that is within me. My emotions and the way I feel on the inside, can determine my external experience of my body. If I believe I am sick, then it is so and I am. If I believe I am getting old, then it is so and I am. I determine the level of my youth, my vitality, my health and how much energy I have in my body. I choose how lit up, passionate and ignited I am about my life or how bored I feel. Yes I am that powerful!

My body is a miraculous machine operating for my highest good all the time. Its functions and malfunctions are related to everything that is going on inside my body, inside my mind and outside my body. I am influenced by my environment, the people I spend time with and the thoughts I think. My healing and empowerment come when I fully realize everything inside of me and outside of me is intricately connected.

I can self heal naturally all ailments and diseases. No illness comes and "attacks me" without my consent and my life style choices up until now. My body is already self healing me in every moment and I just have to help my body along. If I feed my body toxic food, toxic liquids and think toxic thoughts then my body has to work really hard on my self healing. Sometimes my body cannot handle all the garbage coming in and it starts shutting down. My body starts to be in dis-ease. I can continue living with dis-ease inside my body, inside my mind and I will have a pretty crappy experience of life or I can cleanse, heal and rejuvenate my body and thrive. I have to help my body with its healing and cleansing regime. I have to help flush out all the body crap and let go of all the mind crap too.

As a whole being, I now come closer to myself and knowing myself more. I connect to my heart. I connect to my soul. I connect to my intuition. I know my desires, passions and wants. I know myself. I take better care of myself. I love myself more. I see ALL of me and I take care of ALL of me from now on.

I AM WHOLE
AND
I LOVE ME

...

CHAPTER 27

I Am What I Eat

HAVE THE ABILITY TO HAVE AN ULTIMATELY thriving body. I have the ability to heal all sickness. I have the ability to be totally healthy and happy. It comes down to what I eat and how I think. Food is my fuel. If I put crappy fuel in, then my overall sense of well being will be crappy. My mind and brain will feel foggy. My body image will suck and I will feel insecure. I will not have the energy or the stamina to do daily activities let alone go on adventures.

Let food be my medicine and let medicine be my food – this is the oath all doctors swear to but soon forget. Food as our medicine has unfortunately not been on the front lines of our medical or health industry.

It's time to take my health back into my hands. My doctor does not own my health, nor do any of my pharmaceutical drugs. There are ways I can heal my body and have more energy the natural way. The way nature intended. Perhaps plants, greens, fruits and vegetables can help heal me. Perhaps a bunch of vegetables, fruits and green smoothies can make me feel a whole lot better! Perhaps! So I try it the plant path way! I eat raw fruits and veggies as much as possible. I eat whole foods as much as possible.

I cut out the processed crap. I cut out the Genetically Modified Food. I cut out the artificial flavors, colors and enhancements. I cut out the white sugar, the white flour, the white salt and the white processed stuff. I cut out high fructose corn syrup, MSG, aspartame (aka rat poison) and canola oil. I cut out food made in a lab. I cut out food covered in pesticides and sprays. More and more, I cut out food from conventional chemical farming and move towards buying organic. I cut out food coming overseas and shop local as much as possible. I vote with my dollars and support my local small shops, farmers, bakers, craftsman, teachers, healers and leaders in my community.

I cut out food that an animal was harmed for me to eat. I cut out meat as it is very harmful to my body, clogs my arteries, is difficult for my body to digest and is disease causing. I cut out meat slaughtered inhumanly at slaughter houses which is vibrating with the energy of fear, death, torture and deep sadness. I cut out this terror vibration out of my life as much as possible. I cut out dairy as it is acidic, cancer causing and deadly to my body. I become more aware of the harm and torture, animals on this planet endure for our brainwashed society to feed ourselves. I stop pretending the torture does not exist and I awaken to what food and vibration I am putting inside my body.

I eat juicy. I eat food that juices up my mouth and hydrates me instantly. I eat food that is full of water and air content. I eat food that is activated, alive and full of life force. I eat raw as much as possible. I drink lots of liquids. I eat juicy food. I hydrate. Hydrate. Hydrate. I drink spring water. I am really aware where my drinking water comes from. I source where I can get fresh spring drinking water in my area and I go collect my own water or find a source that delivers it. I drink alive full of life force water. Activated alive spring water is the fastest way to purify my blood. When my blood is made up this raw fresh alive earth water, I ground to the earth energy faster and remember my connection. I hang out by rivers, waterfalls and oceans. Water is very healing for my body and the negative ions and ozone that comes off the active moving water, youthens and heals me. I also breathe clean air as much as possible and go into nature to find it.

Raw food is full of oxygen, when I smell my food cooking that is the oxygen leaving the food. Raw food is full of water, as I watch my food shrivel and get smaller on the frying pan, that is the water leaving the food. Raw food is full of life force, as I cook my carrot, I am killing off its life force. If I were to plant that cooked carrot into the ground, it would just rot. If I stuck a raw carrot into the ground, it would grow roots and start growing. The life force is still alive inside the raw carrot. This life force when transferred into my body via raw food gives me energy, nutrients, vitamins, hydration and an extra spring in my step.

Raw food is full of digestive enzymes, so my body does not have to use it's own reserve for digestion. When my body digestive enzymes are not needed for digestion, they spend all their time on my body healing, fixing, cleaning and youthening. The raw food diet is the fastest age reversing, body healing, disease preventing, energy lifestyle because my body actually spends most of its time on healing, cleansing and age reversing while I am eating the most amazing vibrant delicious food.

What is raw food? It's not just carrot sticks and apples. It's elaborate desserts, crackers, breads, dips, sauces, dressings, noodles and the best chocolate ever. I might hear people say, "my body does not like raw food", but I question, what kind of raw food are they eating? How can eating fresh food from a garden, as nature intended not work for them? Yes munching on carrots sticks and eating lots of nuts might be hard to digest. It all depends on how I prepare this delicious fresh food. Once I learn how to do that, then I can feed myself food that is totally flourishing me in every way possible.

I must drink and eat green to be thriving. Green juices and green smoothies. Leafy greens like spinach, cilantro, lettuce, spinach, parsley, bok choy, basil, mint and kale. I could be a junk food raw foodie, by eating only chocolate and raw desserts with lots of nuts. I can be a junk food vegan and junk food vegetarian too. A daily diet of donuts and French fries will be animal cruelty free, but cruel for my human body to eat such harmful food on a regular basis. All in moderation though and I give myself permission to snack on French fries and healthier chips too. To be healthy and thriving I have to add in lots of greens, juices, smoothies, liquids, spring water, raw fruits and vegetables.

I fuel my body with high vibrational foods and liquids and I am a high vibrational being. I give myself permission to be healthy right now. I give myself permission to lose the weight. My issues live in my tissues. What issues can I let go of? Who can I give myself permission to forgive? Can I forgive myself? Where can I let the energy flow through my body again? Where am I blocking my own healthy vibrant body from coming into full expression? Where am I holding back from being the greatest, most healthiest expression of myself?

I give myself permission to let it all go. I give myself permission to thrive. To be the best I can be, in all areas of my life. I give myself permission to shine brighter than I have ever shined before. I recognize that food helps me stuff down my emotions and can give me a sense of comfort in tough times. Sometimes, I might eat to comfort my emotions. I might eat when I am upset, bored, insecure or uncomfortable and food makes me temporarily feel better. Food is connected to my emotions and food makes me feel good for the temporary time being. If I eat crappy food, I will end up feeling more crappy then when I started. My stomach gets bloated, farty and has a hard time digesting crappy food.

I allow myself to see all my issues and I stop stuffing them down with big heavy meals. I let them rise to the surface. I feel them. I acknowledge them. I forgive them. I close my eyes and ask the universe to release them out of my body. I do the work to heal myself. Raw food, green smoothies and fresh juices will help me get these issues to the surface, then it is up to me to get them out of my body forever! If I keep pushing my issues down, then they will just keep surfacing. I will stay in a viscous cycle. So I release them now and forever.

Eating juicy food LIFTS UP my vibration and gives my body more levity. It doesn't allow wounded stuff to get stuffed down so much, so my stuff comes up to be healed. Once it comes up and I heal it, then I am freer and more LIGHTER than I have ever been. I start buzzing and vibrating with so much more raw life force energy and super plant powers.

If I am on a quest for enlightenment, then I eat lighter food and think lighter thoughts. I eat more light and I feel lighter. I let go of heavy dark thoughts and energies and I glow from the inside out. I achieve a state of more light, by eating raw food which is made up of light. I am made of light too and the more I eat light and allow myself to be light, the lighter and brighter I will be.

I AM JUICY

CHAPTER 28

I Eat Life Force

L IFE FORCE IS THE POWER THAT I HAVE within me. It is what breathes and grows me. Life force is the alive energy and the spark in me and in every living thing. Every plant, tree, insect and animal has life force inside. A sunflower seed, for example, has inside it a program for life force to kick in when the seed gets wet. All of a sudden a miraculous set of codes activates and this seed knows to become a giant sunflower plant with hundreds of seeds of its own.

I have this same life force inside me. It grows me taller. Ages me. Grows my hair and nails. Pumps my heart. And when it runs out, I will die. The little life force my dead body still has in it, will continue the program and decompose me back to the soil. Just like a bushel of kale on the counter. When I buy it fresh it is crisp, firm and vibrant. As it sits on the counter, it slowly loses its life force. It wilts. Starts to turn yellow. Looks dry. Starts to get brown. Gets rigid and crispy and decomposes back to the soil. My body and the kale have a similar life cycle. The more life force I eat, the more I will extend my life cycle. The more Eat Juicy Food I eat, the longer I will live. The more life force I have or perceive to have, the more energized and alive I feel. With little life force inside of me, I am tired, lethargic and creeping around half dead in the world.

If I want to have more energy, I eat it. I eat raw fruits, vegetables, greens, plants and leaves that are full of life force. The fresher I pick them and eat them, the more life force they have inside. This life force gets transferred into my body and I feel more energized, healed, cleansed and awesome. Fresh spring water is also full of life force and the more I drink it, the more it will enliven me on a cellular level.

I buy my vegetables from freshly picked markets or grow my own. I avoid grocery produce that has been sitting in warehouses or been transported across the country on trucks for weeks, as its life force energy is so much lower. I buy and eat fresh as much as possible.

EXERCISE: LIFE FORCE IN ACTION

1. I buy 2 bushels of kale. I place Kale #1 wrapped in tea towels in a plastic bag in the fridge or inside a big Tupperware container to preserve the life force. I place Kale #2 on the counter.

2. I now watch both kales daily and see life force in action. Kale #1 in the fridge will stay crispy and fresh much longer because I am preserving the life force. Kale #2 on the counter, out in the elements starts to decompose.

3. I eat Kale #1 from the fridge for my smoothies, juices and salads. I throw the decomposing Kale #2 into my compost. From now on, I eat for life force and I eat fresh. I ideally pick my food from my garden or from sprout trays I am growing inside my house. I grow and eat fresh food as much as possible. It is time to turn my lawn into a garden of food I can eat and feed to others. No more wasting my time, fresh water and weed killer chemicals to keep my lawn looking pretty. It's time to rip out the green turf and plant kale, carrots, tomatoes and herbs instead. The fresher I pick my food, the more surging full of life force it is.

When I replenish the life force batteries inside my body, my life force energy will be overflowing. I will be more vibrant, energized and full of life!

I EAT LIFE FORCE
I EAT JUICY
I LIVE LONG
I AM YOUTHFUL
I AM VIBRANT
I AM AMAZING

...

CHAPTER 29

I Am Thirsty

I AM WHAT I DRINK. MOST LIKELY, I am walking around totally dehydrated and thirsty. My skin shows it. My skin is dull, pimply, dry and resembles a hard wood floor that has lost its shine. My skin is my biggest elimination organ and the last line of defense. So if my skin is looking dull, then I can only imagine how the rest of my organs must be feeling and looking. Toxic and overburdened I am sure. I don't even know what thirsty feels like anymore.

If I am not connected to my body, then I can't really hear my body telling me to drink. I am most likely dried up and my cells are very dry. Dry cells prematurely age and prematurely die. I am slowly aging and killing myself by not drinking enough water and liquids. I am thirsty. At the stem of most sickness is dehydration. Some doctors are quoted as saying, "you are not sick, you are just dehydrated".

So I juice up! I eat more juicy. I add more juicy food into my diet. I drink more spring water. I drink more green smoothies, more green juices and more liquids. Coffee does not count as a liquid, it actually dehydrates me. I make hydration a priority and a major way of my thinking and my living. I Eat Juicy Food more and more now, and hydrate my body with every bite. Juicy is my new lifestyle.

EXERCISE: GETTING HYDRATED

1. I get a glass bottle to carry my spring water around in. I get one portable enough so I can take it with me everywhere. Old juice bottles or mason jars work great. I use glass whenever I can, as it is much healthier for my body. If I use plastic, I use the best quality. I don't buy plastic bottled water. I bring my spring water with me to every event, movie, party or outing. It is always in my car, purse, bag, desk and back pack. Having a big jug will help me gauge how much water I am drinking and will help me track my liquid consumption.

2. I add edible essential oils to my water. This flavors my water to make my hydration a little more exciting. Essential oil water freshens my breath, heals my digestion and alkalines my body. Not all essential oils are made for consumption. Do Terra oils are edible and very good quality. They can heal, activate, energize, freshen and immune boost me. I can order essential oils through Petra, as she is a DoTerra Wellness Advocate.

3. I make daily breakfast green smoothies as my staple morning routine. I can alternate with juices, hot tea elixirs, protein smoothies and various yummy beverages for breakfast too. The green smoothie is my breakfast staple from now on. The power of healing it has on my body and life is miraculous. So I commit to being a Green Smoothie Gangster forever! Sweet or savory green smoothies are my staple food in my new juicy lifestyle.

However **if I am fighting cancer then I avoid sugar and only drink savory smoothies and no fruit green juices.** The smoothies will help me get my toxins out scraping my insides with all the fiber and the green juices will infuse my body with nutrition, vitamins and energy. **If I have digestive gut issues then the green smoothie is going to be better than a green juice for my inflamed digestive track.** I avoid the green juice until my raw inflamed stomach is a bit more healed. Then the green juice will feel much better. The fiber in the green smoothie helps build my gut flora and gives me a healthy digestive system again.

4. I make green juices, veggie and fruit juices. I do it daily or pick a few days of the week as my juicing days. Juicing does take more work, more prep, more produce and more clean up than a green smoothie and the benefits to my body are totally worth it. My body is worth it, so I juice or buy fresh juices a few times per week. I don't buy juice that has been sitting on a shelf, claiming that cold pressing it 12 hours ago still makes this juice fresh. I know that juice is precious and that it loses its life force in every second, so I ask for my juices to be made fresh right in front of me.

5. I reduce the amount of store bought juices I buy. I know fresh is best and most bottled juices are acidic to my stomach. I drink fresh more than store bought. I splash a bottled juice into my water to flavor it up for some variety but I rarely drink it by the glass. I add splashes of juice into my green smoothie mix. I buy good quality juices. I read the ingredients. I feed my body good liquids.

6. I eat lots of juicy fruit. Juicy fruit has fiber which balances the fruit sugars and gives me a perfect energy buzz. Fruit juice can be very high in sugar, can spike my glycemic levels fast and give me a sugar crash. I love juicy apples, watermelon, oranges, mangos, grapes, pomegranates, plums, strawberries and blueberries. I fill my fridge with juicy fruit and make sure I always have a piece to reach for when I am feeling hungry or snackish throughout my day.

7. I eat lots of juicy vegetables and I chew and chew them. I create a personal juicer inside my mouth. I chew to make juice. I no longer swallow big chunks of carrots. They are too hard to digest and might give me a stomach ache. Instead I chew my carrots into juicy little pieces and I swallow them along with the juice I have created inside my mouth. This helps my digestion. Chewing has become old news and I am bringing it back. It's important for my jaw to move and to chew. It makes my teeth and gums stronger and exercises my jaw. Chewing increases saliva flow and saliva is needed to break down and digest my food. If I don't chew, I don't produce saliva and my digestion struggles.

8. I drink spring water. Live raw fresh spring water that will hydrate me so much faster than plastic dead bottled or chlorinated fluorinated tap water. The molecular structure of spring water is understood by my body. It is the key for my lock. My body is very nourished and hydrated by spring water. I find a spring near me or find a delivery service to bring me fresh spring water. The longest living people on the planet have lived around springs. Spring water is my life blood and the liquid that should be flowing through my body for optimal health and connection to my sovereignty.

9. I drink out of glass as much as possible. Plastic can leach chemicals into the water and affect my estrogen levels. Most plastic bottled water is just filtered tap water anyway. I avoid buying plastic bottles and plastic anything as much as possible. Plastic is polluting our world and I can do my part in reducing and recycling my plastic consumption. I bring reusable containers, cloth shopping bags and water bottles with me everywhere. I fill my house with mason jars and cute glasses to inspire my juicy hydration lifestyle.

10. I recognize water is influenced by vibration. Scientists have proven that water will duplicate whatever vibration it is near. If I put the thoughts of hate and fear into my glass, then I will shift the molecular structure to reflect just that. If I put a love, hearts and powerful words on my water bottle then I will influence my water to vibrate at this frequency instead. I focus on putting loving healing energy into my water and my food. My body is also affected by vibration. My body is made up of 80% water. What ever I place on my body or near my body will influence my watery being. If I listen to heavy metal thrasher

music then my body will duplicate this vibration. If I listen to Zen spa music then my body will duplicate this vibration. My watery body will also be influenced by what I surround myself with, the people I spend time with and the environments I put myself into. I am a watery being and my water gets influenced easily. I have choice on how I want to program my body.

11. I drink fresh coconut water when ever possible. Coconuts are the highest sources of natural electrolytes on the planet. Coconut water is the closest liquid to my own human blood and was used in WWII for blood transfusions when human blood was not available. The coconut tree is a miraculous plant with so many amazing uses. I drink coconut water for cleansing, youthening and rehydrating. Coconut water gives me a natural blood transfusion as it cleans and purifies my blood.

I EAT JUICY

CHAPTER 30

I Am A Super Hero

I F I FEEL THE STIRRING IN MY HEART to save the world in some way, then this chapter is for me. As a super hero, I believe there is a "better way" and I am willing to do something to make a difference. I am willing to speak up even when my message might be confrontational to others. I am willing to stand up for what I believe is right and speak my truth.

It can be hard on my heart when those I love reject my truth. It can feel confusing when I get resistance for my desire to help others and make the world a better place. I want to help people. I want to help make their life better, easier and happier. But how can I help people when they reject my help? How can I get my parents to eat healthier so they live longer? How can I get my spouse or my kids to shift to a healthier lifestyle? How can I awaken people to animal cruelty, environmental damage and our world destruction? How can I say it so they hear me?

I have to remember to stay strong in my truth and not take other's opinions personally. Not every hero is seen as a hero immediately, sometimes it takes a little time for others to understand me and understand what I stand for. I must be brave. I must remember my power. I must be willing to be ostracized knowing I am serving a much bigger purpose with my message.

I don't want to lose love or push anyone away, so I also look at how I am delivering my message. Maybe without being fully aware of it, I am bringing judgment energy to those I want to help. If I am a vegan, I perhaps now judge others for eating meat. I see them as wrong and think they should change RIGHT NOW. Yes I want what is best for them and their health, but it is not up to me to judge anyone. Perhaps not too long ago, I too was a meat eater. All I can do is lead by example, inspire and educate those I love. What they choose is up to them. As the saying goes, "I can lead a horse to water, but I cannot make her drink."

I allow everyone to be on their own journey. I let others be. I inspire when I can. I stir up the masses when I am ready. I let people come to me in their time. If I've got something to share or some way to inspire, I let people evolve and awaken in their own time. I can inspire and encourage but I cannot make anyone get there any faster. Sometimes if I push or want it for them so bad, they reject me even more. Sometimes my eagerness for everyone to see the "truth" can push them away. If I am more aware than others, if I eat vegetarian or vegan, if I live a different lifestyle... it can feel threatening to those I love and want to help. It can force them to look at their own life choices and question. Some people don't like to look or make changes and so they will resist me. Other people will be excited, inspired and ready to learn from me. I am not attached to the outcomes I just keeping BEING LOVE and kindness. We are all walking around as wounded beings so we can take things the wrong way very quickly. As super hero out to save the world... love, kindness and compassion are the tools I use to inspire.

I love everyone for where they are. I might not agree with them. I might think I can save their life if only they would listen to me. I might feel frustrated, annoyed and angry at how they are killing themselves. But it is not my place to create someone's destiny. I can only love and inspire them to make better choices and help wake them up from the programming we have all been succumbed to.

I want the world to be a better place. I want to see things getting better in my life and in the world. At the core, I want peace and I want to be happy. I want that happiness for all beings on the planet. I cannot love people but eat animals. I cannot love animals but hate people. I cannot love people and animals and hate my own body. I believe in compassion for all beings, including myself. Sometimes my energy can get very focused on saving out there. Saving the people. Saving the animals. Saving the planet. Saving the ocean. I can forget to save me. Sometimes I can focus so strongly on saving the world and healing other people, and be cruel to my partner and my children. I cannot preach kindness and compassion for animals, and then hate on my fellow humans and super heros just like. We are all fighting for the same cause; An end to suffering; An end to inhumanity; An end to old outdated make no more sense systems;   An end to inequality;   And an end to soul imprisonment. It's time for kindness and compassion for all races and for all living beings.

I cannot pray for peace but judge or hate others. I cannot gossip, speak ill, hate, judge, be jealous, put down or undermine others and call myself an environmentalist, humanitarian, vegan, earth warrior, activist or super hero. It all goes together. I BE LOVE to everyone. I don't judge anyone else. "They are stupid" is such a common belief system of so many. I can get into my ego and think I am smarter or better than someone else. But this ugly and hateful energy is not the answer. I am connected to everyone everywhere, so if I give someone hateful energy, I am also poisoning my own body. So I inspire others but judge them not. Everyone is on their own journey.

Sometimes I won't be understood by my family or peers. That is ok. I am different. Perhaps I am more aware than them. Perhaps I question life a little bit more. Perhaps I have moved from fear and insecurity, to more love and safety. The more I love myself, the less I will seek approval from my family or peers. The more I recognize my worth, the more I am confident in all the choices of my life. My family might come around to my new healthier happier way of thinking or they might not. I love them anyway. I adore them in fact. I express deep gratitude for having a family in this lifetime. They don't have to be like me. They don't have to eat like me. They don't have to think like me. I can love them anyway. I can accept them. I can help them feel more special and better about themselves. Once I create acceptance and fun... then influence, inspiration and change become so much easier.

EXERCISE: USING MY SUPER POWERS OF LOVE & POWERFUL SUBTLE INFLUENCE

I follow these next 2 steps to help all those I want to help with love and inspiration. I try this more subtle approach to helping someone get healthier, happier, more empowered, more inspired and more alive. I no longer have to feel frustrated or disheartened about my lack of influence. These steps will work their own level of magic, in their own time. I just have to keep showing up and letting the magic do its work.

Step 1: I give them a copy of this book and inspire them to open their mind to their own power, divinity and self worth in a fun subtle way.

Step 2: I make them a green smoothie, every morning if that is possible. I don't ask them if they want a smoothie. I make one for myself and out of kindness share my delicious drink with my loves. Even if they drink ½ or they take a few sips. I give them a smoothie every day, making it taste yummy. Very soon their body will crave this drink and their body will be inspired to healthier eating. They will feel better inside their body and better inside their heart. Their life will transform. They will be happier, healthier and more in love with them selves. This is how I will BE LOVE without interference.

Green Smoothies = Love

Giving someone a green smoothie is a ginormous show of love more powerful than I can imagine. I cannot even put value on helping someone's life, giving them energy, helping them lose weight, heal their gut issues, say goodbye to constipation for ever and feel awesome in their body. I just pour them a green smoothie along with pouring mine and offer it to them, acting like it's all no big deal or I deliver it in a mason jar. They drink it. Love it. Feel hooked and feel happier about their life. That is the power of LOVE and a GREEN SMOOTHIE!

I make a green smoothie for myself every morning as it's the GREATEST way I can LOVE myself and offer GRATITUDE to my precious body that is working so hard on my behalf. Loving, healing, replenishing, sustaining and strengthening me in so many ways. I drink green smoothies. Slowly I heal, transform and energize my body and my life.

I am a love warrior. I am a light worker. I am a teacher. I am a parent. I am a guide. I am a bright shiny light for others to follow and learn from in some way. I leave a legacy of myself on this planet. I remind people to love themselves. I remind myself. I don't push anyone into anything. If someone is sick or hurting themselves then I get real with them. Otherwise I let people be. I lead by example. I keep doing what I am doing that is working for me. Eventually people catch up and start asking me for help. I am amazing and I inspire amazing in others.

I am a SUPER HERO! I am an activist. I am an environmentalist. I am a teacher. I am a guru. I am a parent. I am an influencer. I am an earth warrior. I am a water protector. I am a wise owl. I am a smart fox. It is my time of activation on this planet. The planet needs me to fully self express and activate my highest super powers so I may save, heal and halt the extinction of this planet. I am destined for being bigger than I currently am. I am destined to do my part in saving the world in some way. I am destined to make a difference in people's lives. I matter. I am unique. I am special. I am a gift created by the Divine Magnificent All Intelligent Universal Energy. I am the Divine Magnificent All Intelligent Universal Energy in a skin, flesh and watery body. I am grateful to help support others just by being me.

I answer the call and activate myself. Right now. No more playing small. No more shrinking because I will stand out and be called weird. People may ostracize me and I might feel left out. People may no longer understand me but I WON'T BE ALONE. I will find new friends and new people to support the new me. My old friends might come around asking me how to make a green smoothie or how to become a vegan or how to meditate. I focus forward. I let go of the past. I put my energy into the present. I live. I love. I matter.

I lead by example and let people be as they are. I guide people. I help people. I inspire people. I don't force people. They will just resist me and that sucks. Even if they have cancer, I can't push them into juicing or natural medicine if they don't want it. Everyone has their life path to live out. Sometimes it is disheartening to see them dying slowly in front of me knowing their choices might cost them their life but I surrender, inspire as much as I can and then let everyone be on their own journey.

They might be fixated in their way of seeing the world and they might not want to follow me. This can be the most hurtful thing to my soul and my ego. I might feel rejected, unsupported and not as inspired about my life dreams. I might feel defeated. If my own family won't believe in me, then who will? But sometimes, I have to choose my family and sometimes it's not the one I was born into. So I find a tribe of people, a community and clan that I feel at home in and one that supports me in my fullest self expression and evolution as a human on this planet. I shine my light. I am myself. I love my family as they are. I do not make it personal. When I make it personal, I feel lots of pain. So I do not make it personal. They are on their own life path. I am on mine. I am grateful they brought me into this world. Now what amazing thing can I go create? What world changing activity can I put together? How can I serve? This is where I change my focus.

The world has no time for me to rest right now or to feel sorry for myself or feel small, burnt out and defeated. No! I step it up right now! The world needs me! Needs my voice to speak up for what is not right. The world needs me to stand up for my rights as a sovereign human on this planet. The world needs me now. No more sleeping. Time to wake up, throw off the covers and put my super hero costume on. It's time to make a bigger difference on this planet.

I ABSOLUTELY MATTER
MY VOICE TOTALLY MATTERS
ALL MY PASSION MATTERS
WHAT I STAND FOR MATTERS
I AM AMAZING
I CARE
I MAKE A DIFFERENCE IN PEOPLE'S LIVES
I AM A SUPER HERO

...

CHAPTER 31

I Am A Parent

I F I AM A PARENT OR HAVE kids in my life who I want to create an amazing connection with, then this chapter is for me. As a parent I might be busy and not have much time for my kids. I might be working long hours. Have 2 jobs. Maybe I'm a single parent and have to do this all on my own. Juggle my kids, my work, housework, eating, cooking, nurturing, socializing, smiling and pretending I have it all together. My time with my kids might be mainly spent "taking care of their main needs" and I might not have much time to really "play" with them. I am actually quite grateful, when they are playing and occupying themselves. So how can I create more love, connection, respect and adoration with my kids? How can I juggle all I have to do and still show up as a rock star amazing parent? How can I open myself up to more joy and allow my kids to actually help heal me?

It's time to truly play with my kids. Time to start enjoying life through their eyes of joy and wonder. Time to start really listening to them and to their view of life. Open. No judgment.

Only encouragement and "tell me more". I am a safe space for my kids to talk to me – about anything. I prefer to have my child tell me their worst nightmares and problems, then hide things from me. I am here to guide and lead the way for my child. I am here to help guide them to their intuition and to their heart's deepest longing and mission. I don't put my issues and life dreams of "what I desire them to be" on them. I let them be free. Free to choose their destiny. Free to follow their heart and use their inner compass as a guide for life.

The faster I can help my child connect to their inner compass, the faster I assure their inner power will remain really strong. This inner connection and inner power will guide them to their greatest full self expression and potential on this planet. It will help guide them to be the very best version of themselves. This is the greatest gift I can give my child, to help guide them to their highest self so they feel more connected, grounded and at peace in their life journey. I continue reminding my child of their greatness, enoughness, self worth, self love and self empowerment.

Obviously I have to cultivate all this within me first, before I can teach my child. That is why I have been cultivating all this with every word I have been reading in this book. I cannot teach self love to my child if I don't have self love for myself. My child will feel the incongruence. My child watches my actions and learns from my behaviors. If I want to have a healthy thriving child, I must be healthy and thriving myself.

Now back to the playing! How often am I allowing myself to bubble over in giggles with my kids? How often can I let it all go, roll around on the floor, laugh and BE IN THE MOMENT? In THIS present moment. Not thinking about the office. Not thinking about what to make for dinner. Not thinking about the piles of laundry. Be present in this moment. Right here. Right now. Fully present with my kids.

EXERCISE 1: PLAY TIME

1. I set a timer or create a time frame to fully commit to play. No distractions. No thinking about something else. I play full out. What ever my kids want to play. Hide and seek. Board games. Tickle fights. Pillow fights. I giggle. I dream. I imagine. I play make believe. I drink imaginary tea from little cups. I look for fairies in the garden. I am inspired. I am giddy. I am lighter. I see the world with more wonder. I see the world with more innocence. I see the world with more play. I see myself as more flexible and fun. I allow myself to see the world from my child's eyes. I humble myself to my child's wisdom, to their deep inner connection and to their own invincibility. I let myself be reminded of the innocence I once had. I remember, I too am invincible and wonder filled, if I choose to be.

I can change, morph and release anything that is no longer serving me. I can play. I can be young. I can be innocent. I can be childlike. I get to choose.

EXERCISE 2: FAMILY TIME

A great gift I can give my children, is to create family time for a few hours 1 night per week as we create important quality time together. All kids want their mom and dad to be happy and to have a safe loving home life.

Kids want to play with their parents. They feel safe seeing their whole family together and happily playing with each other. I love board games! My kids love them! Board games create connection. Video games will not work here.

1. I pick the day and then plan my week with this important appointment that I keep.

2. I create routine around this important event to show my kids and myself that this matters. Because it does. I am committed to my word of spending quality time with my family.

3. We learn to play together and relate to each other. We laugh with each other and connect to each other on a deeper more intimate level. We create a more solid family unit.

4. We sit at the dining room table and play a board game. I set the clock for 2 hours. 2 hours of quality uninterrupted time. No texting. No checking the sport scores. No chatting on the phone. Quality time with my kids.

5. I find the most fun board games. I get a few and alternate. I create time where the family unit laughs and enjoys each other. We eat healthy popcorn. We listen to fun music. We drink fizzy healthy drinks. We create dress up time. We have fun. We are wild. I use my imagination and add more fun in. I am open. I am kind. I create more LOVE!

LOVE & CONNECTION
1 NIGHT
2 HOURS EVERY WEEK
COMMITTED TIME FRAME
FUN & GIGGLES
LOVE & CONNECTION

I AM A GHOST
DRIVING A MEAT COVERED SKELETON
MADE OF STARDUST
RIDING A FLOATING ROCK
THROUGH OUT OUTER SPACE

...

CHAPTER 32

A Final Love Note From My Soul

I AM MADE OF STARDUST. EVERYTHING I AM and everything in the universe and on earth originated from stardust. It continually floats through me even today. It directly connects me to the universe and makes up over 93% of my body. I am impermanent. My body is made up of remnants of stars and massive explosions of galaxies. The plants are made of stardust too and I eat them. This stardust swirls in and around my body and is in every thing I see. My body will dissolve into stardust when I die. If I believe in reincarnation, then a new stardust body will be created around my soul. When I reincarnate back to earth, I can come with all the baggage, wounds and crap from this lifetime or I can heal this lifetime of crap now! I can awaken to my greatness now! I can choose to let go of all my negative limiting beliefs! I can choose to focus on the positive and empowering ones! I can choose to see my FULL power!

I am a sparkly piece of Divine Cosmic Universal Energy living inside a skin bag. Once the life force energy of my skin bag runs out, I will return to the Cosmos. Perhaps I will reincarnate and return back to earth into another skin bag, human or animal or perhaps I will not. I am energy. The same energy that surges through me, surges through every living thing. My energy is infinite. I am the same as everyone else, just my skin bag looks different. I am a spark of life using this skin bag as a spaceship to travel around on earth. I look in the mirror and see past this body and see my true divine spark.

I look at others and see past their skin bag bodies and see their true divine spark. We are all the same on the inside. I am the same spark as an animal and the same spark as my neighbor. The faster I see my brothers, sisters and animal friends like me, the faster I will create peace, love and justice on this planet. We are all doing the best we can. We are all adjusting and adapting to living as a human on this planet. We all have the same fears, insecurities and hopes. I accept my power and inspire others to accept theirs. I am powerful. I am amazing. I love my body. I love my life. I love myself. I don't know how long I have on this earth, so....

I CHOOSE TO MAKE THIS LIFETIME COUNT!

CHAPTER 33

A Final Love Note From Petra

I HAVE LIVED ON THE ISLAND OF MAUI, Hawaii previous to Bali, for 5 years. I lived magically off the grid in conscious communities eating food off the land, swimming naked in private waterfalls and walking barefoot as much as possible. In Hawaiian thinking (and as you know my own), words have MANA (spiritual and divine power) and ALOHA and MAHALO are two of the most sacred and powerful. Two magical meanings of these words that I discovered are:

Aloha means hello I see the Divine in you. Hawaiians say hello by coming together and sharing breath. Aloha is the invocation of that breath to be welcomed in to our space. Mahalo means thank you for showing me the Divinity (breath) that dwells in you and may you be blessed in Divine breath forever.

~ Mahalo Dear Reader! Mahalo for reading this book and empowering yourself ~

I have always been drawn to the 'something more out there' curious calling. Without my "intent", the universe has been guiding my path all along. 15 years ago my mom was diagnosed with cancer and died within 3 months.   My best friend, weekend playmate and daily telephone confidant was gone. At the time I was unaware, that her death would launch me on a very accelerated learning, growing, expanding and enlightening journey. I have been fortunate to commune, learn from and become allies with some of the most super hero teachers on the planet. Conscious awake healthy vibrant age reversing mind awakening sovereign beings just like you and me!

I spent these past 15 years with lots of spiritual and health books, with amazing teachers, in the most empowering schools, lived off the grid in conscious communities, made home in elaborate tree houses and hobbit fairy houses on incredible organic jungle farms, traveled the world, ripped shreds of old unserving crap off of me, healed my heart and my soul, learned to adore myself on a totally new level, became more empowered and connected to myself, sat in many circles with shamans, priestesses, healers and angelic beings, launched myself into full self expression teaching natural health, raw food, natural healing, cleansing, detox, digestion, age reversing, longevity, natural beauty, self empowerment, self love, mindfulness and cancer healing to the world, impacted many lives with my teachings and created home in two of the most magical places on earth, Maui Hawaii and Bali Indonesia.

I have been on a diligent path. I believe I have been put on this planet to bring more light to humanity and to lead the Super Human Love Warriors in a World Peace Revolution and ensure WE WIN. This book is one tool to ensure we succeed in this mission. May you be a brighter, lighter, happier, healthier and more empowered super human for reading it and may you spread more love, light and healing on this planet as a result.

I am a constant learner and a seeker of truth, empowerment and sovereignty. If you are the same, then explore what makes your heart come alive, seek out what stirs your passion and keep learning!

So much love and aloha,
Petra

WE ARE
SUPER HUMAN LOVE WARRIORS
WE GO IN PEACE
WE ARE FIERCE IN LOVE
WE RALLY FOR A WORLD PEACE REVOLUTION
WE WIN

...

PETRA'S FAVOURITE TEACHERS

ONE OF MY FAVORITE TEACHERS OF SPIRITUALITY, power of language and life accountability is **Louise Hay**. She owns the biggest spiritual publishing house, has authored many amazing books and has up leveled my life in so many ways by listening to her audio books. I love making my vehicle and all travel trips my personal classroom by listening to audio books. I invite you to read her book *You Can Heal Your Life* as a must on your evolution journey, it is my all time favorite book. I learned much about self love, mirror work, affirmations and my inner child from Louise Hay and am blessed to embody her teachings daily.

I first learned about my inner child from another favorite guru, mentor and massively impactful teacher on my spiritual journey **Wayne Dyer**. A Maui based author and the father of spirituality, his audio books were my automobile classroom. I listened to his audio wisdom on all my world journeys and highly recommend you do the same. Listening to him speak to me via audio with his kind, calm, wisdom filled voice was my favorite most empowering activity for many years.

I love **Marianne Williamson**, listening to her speak live or on audio elevates me every time. You can find an audio recording of her book *A Return To Love* on YouTube. It is a MUST and can bring so much more BE LOVE into your heart and shift your perspective on the way you see the world. Her teachings are based on *A Course In Miracles* and she is the one who reminded me that asking for a miracle was my birthright.

David Wolfe, is my raw food, spring water and super food super hero! This man is so brilliant and knows his stuff. He inspired me to super hero level health, the possibility of longevity and expanded my mind awareness so much. I love listening to him speak, love reading all his books and love hearing about the latest revolutionary health discovery kick he is on. I've organized events for him in Vancouver, got him on press and stayed with him at his Hawaii Noni Land Property. I'm proud of him for speaking his truth, not conforming to the masses and standing for our human sovereignty. I am honored to call him my friend.

Daniel Vitalis, activated my spring water obsession, love of medicinal mushrooms, elixir medicines and awakened me to the misguided fabricated history and brainwashing we as humans have endured. I first learned about him from another raw food super hero **Steve Prussack**, who hosted Raw Vegan Radio for many years and is now the Juice Guru. I spent countless hours listening to all Raw Vegan Podcasts and watching all of Daniel's

YouTube Videos on spring water, wild plant foraging and edible medicinal mushrooms. I reached out to him on a radio show and had the pleasure of organizing his Vancouver events and doing retreats with him. He started www.FindASpring.com, which I promote all over the world to search for fresh water springs in your area. I use this website on all my world travels as I only drink spring water for the past 8 years.

Brian Clement, doctor and teacher at the Hippocrates Natural Healing Institute in Florida, embodies self healing and disease reversal. He has shown me how possible it is for us to heal from anything. His center specializes in disease reversal especially cancer and education. He studied with Ann Wigmore and I've been to many of his events. His books, teachings, lectures and videos are awesome and worth checking out.

Ann Wigmore, I found when I was researching how to heal my mom of cancer naturally. She is the original founder of Hippocrates Healing centers. She was my first glimpse into the power of nutrition, raw food and the possibility that the body can reverse sickness and heal itself naturally. She healed herself and even reversed her grey hair through chlorophyll, wheat grass and raw food nutrition. She is one of the pioneers of the natural health movement along with **Rudolf Steiner, Norman Walker & Victoria Boutenko** – more of my favorite teachers.

Café Gratitude, Mathew & Terces Engelhart and **Café Attitude** Jeanne Angelheart & Virginia, awakened another level of self love, self empowerment and self mastery within me. Café Gratitude is an empire of amazing raw food and conscious life creating restaurants, books and farms filled with intention, love and purpose. I am blessed to have learned the art of BE LOVE, personally from this power couple. Café Attitude is an open mic, fresh off the land restaurant and magical spot on Maui run by a Queen that only the locals and those who are destined attend. I am blessed it was my weekly hang out spot, that infused my body with so much high vibrational empowering music, uplevelling language and great times. I learned the art of Queendom from the best and cherish my Maui family immensely. Another incredible Maui teacher to me is my friend **Amrita Nectar**, who I call the wizard and I am in deep gratitude for his abilities to up level my language, sever my limitations and remind me of my great power.

Don Miguel Ruiz book *The Four Agreements* are my guiding principles. Read them. Embody them.

Landmark Educational Seminars, empowered my mind and helped me pop out of the bubble of illusion. I believe this school is a gift to humanity. Take the Level 1 weekend course and prepare for an awakening.

More Teachers I LOVE: Caroline Myss, David Deida, Alison Armstrong, Abraham, Yogi Bhajan, Brendon Burchard, David Ike, Sacred Ayahuasca Ceremonies, Native American Teepee Ceremonies, Goddess Gatherings, Priestess Temple of Ashland, Sacred Mount Shasta, Vortex Powerful Sedona, Beloved Bali, Momma Maui, Sacred Breath Work, Kundalini Yoga, Kirtan Music, Conscious Festivals, Ecstatic Dance, Mindfulness Training, My Haluska Family who I choose to BE LOVE for the most, Movies like (Food Matters, Thrive, Food Inc., The Sugar Film, Fat Sick and Nearly Dead, What the Bleep Do We Know), Wisdom Guidance Card Decks by Alana Fairchild and so much more.

I AM AMAZING
I AM POWERFUL
I AM INFINITE
I AM ENOUGH

...

Petra EatJuicy, is a Super Hero Level Holistic Health Coach, Detox Expert, Author, Raw Food Chef, Theta Healing Practitioner, Yogini & Juicy Lifestyle Activist. She travels the world speaking, teaching and coaching about natural eating, self healing, mindfulness, self love and personal empowerment. She and her team tour the world empowering people, to take their health into their own hands by joining Green Smoothie Gangster Health Challenge...cuz it works. She lives in Bali, Indonesia and Maui, Hawaii.

Check out her amazing online coaching programs to reverse cancer, heal your gut, lose weight without counting calories and live your most vibrant self expressed life.

www.EatJuicy.com
www.GreenSmoothieGangster.com

www.Facebook.com/PetraEatJuicyTV
www.Youtube.com/PetraEatJuicy
www.Instagram.com/PetraEatJuicy

We are a Gang
Healing the Planet

Join Us!

eat juicy.com

love your life

Green Smoothie Gangster.com

Printed in Great Britain
by Amazon

54676429R00127